THE *ultimate*
ONE-PAN OVEN COOKBOOK

THE *ultimate*
ONE-PAN OVEN COOKBOOK

Complete Meals Using Just Your Sheet Pan,
Dutch Oven, Roasting Pan *and More*

JULIA KONOVALOVA

Creator of Imagelicious

PAGE STREET
PUBLISHING CO.

For Alan and Lana, my two loves

CONTENTS

Introduction

I wish I could start this intro by writing a story about making cookies with my mom for Santa when I was a child. Or, perhaps, writing about slicing strawberries, still warm from the sun, with my grandma at the cottage and making jams when I was nine. But that never happened. Food and childhood intertwine in my mind. Smells and flavors conjure long-forgotten memories and nostalgic moments that I'm mostly sure never even happened. Yet, I don't have many stories about actually cooking when I was little. I spent hours in the kitchen observing and rarely participating.

By the time I became a teenager and subsequently moved to Canada from Russia, I knew a lot about cooking without actually cooking much. If I found myself suddenly without any parental supervision in a kitchen, I'd delve right away into complicated dishes. Beef and mushroom stroganoff and cream puffs were some of the first recipes I made. For almost a decade after, I spent hours, sometimes days, cooking and conjuring fancy and elaborate meals. No wonder I survived mostly on sandwiches in between my cooking feats.

Once I got married, my cooking philosophy changed a lot. I stopped with intricate and complicated and turned to simple, yet flavorful. That's when I discovered oven cooking, got comfortable in the kitchen and taught myself to cook again. I hope that this book will do just that—ease anxiety about cooking, help get food on the table and create time to spend with your family instead of at the stove stirring pots and pans for hours.

Cooking in the oven isn't quick, and you won't have dinner on the table 30 minutes after coming home—mostly because preheating the oven to the correct temperature takes a long time. But waiting for the oven to heat up is when the bulk of food preparation is done, and once everything is chopped and mixed and seasoned, the oven does the rest. You get to have a glass of wine or watch a TV show or help the kids with homework. There's no stirring pots, no cleaning the stove or grease-splattered counters, although I usually have a rice cooker going or buckwheat cooking to add to the meal.

If you worry that oven cooking is just for cold winter months, I'd like to assure you—it's not. All the recipes in this cookbook have been developed and tested over and over again during a very hot summer. The beauty of cooking in the oven, especially making complete meals in one pan, is that you don't have to actually be in the kitchen while the food is roasting or baking. So, even though the kitchen will most likely get hot from the oven, you won't! Cooking in the oven means you will get a delicious and wholesome meal with little hands-on cooking time and a lot of flavor!

Cooking Notes

For years I struggled with cooking in my fancy oven. Renovating my kitchen, I spent weeks, if not months, choosing the stove I wanted. In the end, I chose something relatively high-end with nothing digital. Recipe after recipe, I was perplexed—30 minutes to cook chicken in the oven? Forget about it! It wouldn't be done after 50 minutes or 75. I had to allocate at least 1½ hours for baking or roasting a simple chicken breast.

Finally, I knew I had to deal with this issue and hire someone to look at, and possibly recalibrate, my oven. In a last-minute decision, I chose to try something else before spending hundreds of dollars on the assessment. I bought a new oven thermometer and a meat thermometer. I had a few oven thermometers in the past, usually purchased on an impulse at a grocery store. They never worked properly. My current meat thermometer seemed okay but it was old and cheap, and I wanted a change. After some research, I found two products and decided to give them a try. Neither were that expensive. The oven thermometer cost about fifteen dollars on Amazon and was recommended by many people and culinary sites. The meat thermometer cost a bit more, but at 35 dollars on Amazon, it was still not a huge investment.

Once I received my new toys, I started testing them. To my astonishment, it turned out that my oven was perfectly calibrated, almost to a degree. It just took a really, really long time to preheat to the required temperature. I thought I was putting my roasting pans filled with food into a 350°F (176°C) preheated oven when in reality it was only 300°F (149°C). No wonder everything took two or even three times longer to cook. My new meat thermometer also surprised me. There was a difference of 20 degrees between my old and new gadgets. Apparently I had been overcooking meats for years.

When cooking in the oven, it's really important to know how your oven actually works. Some run colder, some hotter. Five degrees may not make a difference in cooking time but 10 to 15 degrees might. I highly recommend investing in an oven thermometer, as well as a meat thermometer, to make sure that all meats are cooked to their safe internal temperatures.

Unlike cooking temperature, which needs to be precise, seasonings are very individual. Contrary to popular chef teachings, I don't use a lot of salt in my cooking, and although I included some measurement of salt in my recipes, the saltiness of the food is a personal preference. For most people, the amount of salt that I use is not enough, so make sure to add salt to your taste. I find that many meats and even vegetables have enough natural sodium in them that there's no need for all the salt. It wasn't a quick change; I gradually reduced my salt intake over the years. Now, I let the natural flavors of the ingredients speak.

I also like to have a little spicy kick in my food, so I use chili powder and cayenne pepper often. My mom, on the other hand, can taste even a quarter teaspoon of black pepper and considers it spicy. Just like with the salt, feel free to omit the pepper if you don't like heat or increase it for a spicier dish. If you are just starting out on your cooking journey, try the seasonings I list in my recipes, and then adjust to your taste when you cook something again. It's important to develop your own palate, and it will happen over time. If I don't have time to add the seasonings and herbs I list in the recipe, or if I run out of some of them, I use my favorite secret ingredient—Mrs. Dash seasoning. It's a blend of many spices and herbs that adds a wonderful savory depth of flavor to any dish. You can find it at almost any grocery store, or buy it online.

In many of the recipes, I add notes for substitution of ingredients: parsley instead of cilantro or dill. Apples or no apples. Little variations to flavors. Feel free to experiment in the kitchen. If you don't like broccoli, use cauliflower, or change up trout and use salmon instead. Add garlic. Omit onion. All these changes, of course, will result in a different flavor profile but this is how new recipes are created. I strongly believe in being creative in the kitchen. It's what makes cooking fun and relaxing instead of stressful. To me, cooking isn't a chore—well, sometimes it is. But most of the time I love the creativity that cooking allows me to explore.

Oven-Made Breakfasts

Breakfast (or brunch) is my favorite meal of the day. So much so that I actually had a brunch wedding reception as opposed to the traditional dinner. There's something about steaming cups of tea and pots of coffee, the smell of crispy bacon and the sound of butter melting and foaming in the pan as it waits for the eggs. I love cooking breakfast on the weekends when there's no rush to get the food on the table. I can sip my coffee and chop potatoes, flip pancakes or check on whatever is baking in the oven.

When I feel lazy, I turn to my oven. Making breakfast in the oven means that there are fewer pans to wash and no grease-splattered counters to wipe. It means you can enjoy a few extra minutes of quiet (if it's ever quiet in your household in the morning) or watch a show or play with your child. Oven breakfasts aren't just bread puddings or frittatas. I use my oven to make Oven-Baked Maple-Sriracha Bacon (page 27)—it's easy, there's almost no cleanup and all the fat drains to the pan, making it just a tiny bit healthier. I use the heat of the oven to make Millet Porridge with Cranberries (page 20). I even "boil" eggs in the oven—Easy Oven-Boiled Eggs (page 31)—to have for breakfasts or for snacks throughout the week.

Using your oven to make breakfast means you can very easily invite people over for brunch—my favorite way of entertaining friends. I usually have fruit, veggies, cheese and bread on the table, and something cooking in the oven. You get to spend time with friends and family without cooking eggs to order or flipping pancakes. Prepare my Make-Ahead Leek and Goat Cheese Strata (page 15) the evening before and just pop it in the oven in the morning. Or impress your guests with a tray of Mango-Chili French Toast (page 24).

Sheet Pan Breakfast WITH BACON, POTATOES AND MUSHROOMS

Making the whole breakfast on one sheet pan in the oven means that there's almost no cleanup in the end. You don't have to battle with splattering bacon grease while stirring potato hash and making sure that the eggs aren't overdone. Everything is cooked on one pan in the oven and comes out hot at the same time. And if you have more people coming over for breakfast, then just double the ingredients and use two sheet pans. Everything will still cook at the same time, and everyone will get to enjoy their delicious and hot breakfast together. In this recipe, hearty and earthy mushrooms mingle with crispy bacon and fragrant herbs and spices. You get a delicious potato hash, eggs and toast, all cooked together on just one sheet pan.

Serves 2 to 4

2 large potatoes (about 1–1½ lbs [450–680 g] total)

½ large onion

½ lb (227 g) sliced mushrooms

1 tsp dried thyme

½ tsp dried rosemary

½ tsp chili powder

½ tsp salt

1 tbsp (15 ml) olive oil

4 pieces bacon

4 eggs

2 slices bread

2 tbsp (5 g) chopped parsley

½ pint (160 g) cherry tomatoes

Salt and pepper for serving

Preheat the oven to 425°F (218°C). While the oven is preheating, dice the potatoes into ¼-inch (6-mm) cubes and finely chop the onion. Place the diced potatoes and onions onto a rimmed baking sheet. I use one that is 13 x 17 inches (33 x 43 cm). Add the mushrooms, all the spices and olive oil; mix really well. I prefer using my hands to mix, but make sure to wash them well as the chili powder will make your eyes sting.

Spread the potato-mushroom mixture in one layer on the sheet pan. Cut the bacon into 1- to 2-inch (2.5- to 5-cm) pieces, and scatter them all over the potatoes. Bake for about 35 to 40 minutes, or until the potatoes are cooked through.

After the potatoes are cooked, take the sheet pan out of the oven and move potatoes to make four wells. Check that there's enough grease in those wells from the olive oil and bacon fat; if your baking sheet isn't nonstick, you might need to add a few drops of oil to the wells. Carefully crack an egg into each well.

Place pieces of bread, cut diagonally, onto the potatoes and return the pan to the oven. Bake for 10 minutes for runny egg yolks. If you prefer egg yolks to be fully cooked and hard, then bake for another 5 to 10 minutes to reach desired doneness.

Serve with chopped parsley, halved or quartered cherry tomatoes and extra salt and cracked black pepper to taste.

Make-Ahead Leek and
Goat Cheese Strata

I discovered stratas almost a decade ago, and since then, they have been a staple for all the brunches that I host. The basic idea is that bread is covered with an egg and milk mixture, some kind of filling (vegetables, cheese, meat, fish) and then refrigerated overnight. In the morning, you just pop the whole tray in the oven, and a hot bubbling breakfast is ready when the guests arrive. No need to stand at the stove and cook eggs to order. In this particular case, I used leeks, spinach and goat cheese as my filling. I love using brioche or challah as a base for the strata, as they provide a subtle sweetness that contrasts well with the tangy and salty cheese.

Serves 6 to 8

1 tsp salted or unsalted butter

5–6 cups (300–350 g) cubed challah or brioche (1–2-inch [2.5–5-cm] cubes)

1 leek, white and light green parts only

1 tbsp (15 ml) olive oil

4 cups (120 g) baby spinach

½ tsp chili flakes

1 small log (3.5 oz [100 g]) goat cheese

5 eggs

1⅓ cups (315 ml) milk

1 tbsp (15 ml) Dijon mustard

½ tsp salt, or more to taste

½ tsp pepper

½ mozzarella ball, shredded (about 1 cup [130 g])

Chopped dill for serving (optional)

Do not preheat the oven. Butter a 9 x 13-inch (23 x 33-cm) roasting pan and cover the bottom with the cubes of challah or brioche, trying to make sure that they are in a single layer.

Wash the leek really well between the layers to make sure that there are no grains of dirt. Slice it in half lengthwise, and slice each part into thin half circles. Heat the olive oil in a medium or large pan over medium heat, add the sliced leeks and cook for about 5 minutes, stirring occasionally, until the leeks start to soften. Add spinach and chili flakes; cook until the spinach is wilted.

Evenly spread the leek–spinach mixture over the bread. Crumble the goat cheese and sprinkle it over the bread and leeks.

In a large bowl, whisk the eggs and milk together until smooth. Add the mustard, salt and pepper, and mix well. Pour the egg mixture over the bread, making sure that all the bread is covered. Top with shredded mozzarella, cover with foil and refrigerate overnight or for at least 6 hours.

In the morning, take the strata out of the fridge and let it come to room temperature while the oven is heating. Preheat the oven to 350°F (176°C). Place the strata in the oven still covered for 15 minutes. After the initial 15 minutes, take the foil off and bake for another 30 minutes or until the eggs are fully cooked and the strata is firm. I love the combination of goat cheese and dill, so I usually serve it sprinkled with chopped dill.

Note: Technically, a few-days-old bread is supposed to be used for strata, but I have used both fresh and stale bread with very similar results.

EASY CRANBERRY-PECAN *Granola*

I love eating granola with Greek yogurt or just plain yogurt for breakfast. For quite a few months I was buying a really delicious granola and enjoying it until one day I looked at the nutrition information. It turned out that my breakfast wasn't as healthy as I thought—it was actually full of sugars and oils. This recipe uses only a couple of tablespoons of maple syrup and a bit of coconut oil, making the granola much healthier, yet still delicious.

Makes 2 ½ cups (310 g)

1½ cups (120 g) rolled oats

½ cup (75 g) dried cranberries

½ cup (60 g) chopped pecans

2 tsp (5 g) cinnamon

½ tsp nutmeg

2 tbsp (30 ml) maple syrup

1 tbsp (15 g) coconut oil

Preheat the oven to 375°F (190°C). Scatter the oats, cranberries and pecans on a nonstick 11 x 17-inch (28 x 43-cm) or larger baking sheet. Sprinkle with cinnamon and nutmeg, and mix well.

Drizzle the maple syrup and melted coconut oil over all the oats. Mix well using a spatula.

Bake for 10 minutes. Cool and enjoy.

Note: This recipe makes a very lightly sweetened granola. You can use more maple syrup if you prefer sweeter granola. You can also use honey or agave syrup if you like. The resulting granola will be loose and without big clusters.

RICOTTA *Cheesecake Pancakes*

In Russia, one of the most popular weekend breakfasts is farmer cheese pancakes, called *syrniki*. They are usually made with farmer cheese, egg, a touch of sugar and just a little bit of flour. This recipe is a variation of my childhood favorite. I use ricotta in place of farmer cheese now almost exclusively, as it's a lot easier to find in stores. Instead of making individual pancakes and frying them on the stove, the batter is poured into a sheet pan and baked in the oven. The resulting concoction tastes like a mix between a regular pancake and a light ricotta cheesecake. It's soft and creamy inside and the little ripples of jam add delicious contrast to the texture.

Serves 6

PANCAKE BATTER
1 tub (10.5 oz [300 g]) ricotta

3 large eggs

1 cup (235 ml) milk

½ cup (120 ml) orange juice

¼ cup (55 g) light brown sugar

1¼ cups (155 g) all-purpose flour

½ cup (40 g) quick-cooking oats

¾ tsp cinnamon

¾ tsp baking powder

Pinch of salt

Butter or oil, and a bit of flour for the pan

TOPPING
¼ cup (60 ml) jam—blueberry, black currant or your favorite

1 tbsp (15 ml) orange juice (optional)

Maple syrup for serving

Preheat the oven to 350°F (176°C). In a large bowl, combine the ricotta, eggs, milk and orange juice. Whisk until smooth. Add the rest of the dry ingredients—sugar, flour, oats, cinnamon, baking powder, salt—and mix until just incorporated. Do not overmix. It's fine if the mixture is lumpy.

Grease a 13 x 9-inch (33 x 23-cm) sheet pan. Sprinkle with a bit of flour and shake to make sure that the pan is covered. Shake the excess flour out. Spread the prepared pancake mixture evenly inside the sheet pan.

If the jam you are using is too thick, then mix it together with 1 tablespoon (15 ml) of orange juice. Dot the jam over the pancake batter and, using the tip of a knife, swirl it around to create a marble effect.

Bake in the preheated oven for 40 to 45 minutes. Cut into squares, and serve hot with maple syrup.

Millet Porridge WITH CRANBERRIES

When I was growing up, porridge was a staple on our breakfast table. I loved all kinds of porridges: oatmeal, cream of wheat, buckwheat, rice. Millet porridge was my favorite, probably because it was quite rare that my mom made it. Millet notoriously takes a long time to cook, and standing in front of the stove and stirring for an hour wasn't something my mom was able to do often. I wish she knew about this amazing way of cooking millet porridge in the oven. You just mix all the ingredients, stick the little pots in the oven and forget about them until they're done. You don't even need to preheat the oven! The result is creamy and delicious, slightly sweetened with brown sugar and dried fruit. I love serving it with extra Baked Milk (page 158).

Makes 1 serving

¼ cup (50 g) millet

½ tsp light or dark brown sugar

1 tbsp (10 g) dried cranberries

Pinch of salt

¾ cup (175 ml) milk (or Baked Milk [page 158])

½ tsp butter for serving (optional)

About ¼ cup (60 ml) milk for serving (optional)

Add all the ingredients to a small ceramic pot and cover with a lid. French onion soup pots are great for this. You need something with more than 8.5-ounce (250-ml) capacity.

Place the pot onto a baking sheet covered with foil or parchment paper. This is important, as if you have a smaller pot there will most likely be spillovers, and parchment paper will help with cleanup.

Place the baking sheet with the little pot into a cold oven and turn it on to 350°F (176°C). Cook for 1 hour.

Once the millet porridge is cooked, take the pot out of the oven, remove the lid and mix everything with a spoon. Add butter, if using, and a little bit of milk to make it creamy.

Options: Try this with dried currants, raisins, dried cherries or chopped prunes. Cinnamon is also a great addition to this porridge.

Baked Smoked Salmon AND GOAT CHEESE EGG-IN-A-HOLE TWO WAYS

I love having people over for brunch. It's fun and less stressful than cooking a formal dinner. I usually serve a cheese platter with crackers, make a simple waffle batter in advance, cook waffles right at the dining table and serve some kind of an egg dish that I don't have to fry to order. In most cases, I make a strata (try my Make-Ahead Leek and Goat Cheese Strata on page 15) or a tray of Baked Smoked Salmon and Goat Cheese Egg-in-a-Hole Two Ways, as they are a cinch to prepare and only take a few minutes to cook. Making eggs this way means that I don't have to spend time in the kitchen instead of socializing with my friends and family. Adding smoked salmon and goat cheese makes the brunch feel special, and even a little bit festive.

Serves 2 to 4

2 tsp (10 g) butter

4 slices whole wheat sandwich bread

1 tsp vegetable oil

2 slices (about 1 oz [30 g]) smoked salmon, divided

1 oz (30 g) goat cheese, crumbled, divided

2 tsp (6 g) capers, chopped

4 eggs

Salt and pepper to taste

Preheat the oven to 425°F (218°C). Lightly butter each slice of bread. Cut out the center of the bread slices, leaving about ½ inch (1.3 cm) of the crusts to create a hollow square. Place the bread slices and the cut-out centers of bread, buttered-side up, on a nonstick baking sheet. Drizzle the oil into each hole.

For the first style of toasts, chop half of the smoked salmon into small pieces and add to a small bowl. Add half the crumbled goat cheese, half the capers and two eggs to the bowl. Mix well with a fork. Pour the mixture into the holes of two bread slices.

For the second style of toasts, cut the smoked salmon slice in half and layer at the bottom of each remaining bread slice hole. The smoked salmon should cover most of it. Top it with the remaining crumbled goat cheese and chopped capers. Carefully crack the egg on top of the goat cheese, making sure that the yolk remains whole.

Bake in the oven: 12 minutes for medium eggs or 9 to 10 minutes for runnier eggs.

Note: Feel free to double or triple the ingredients to make more toasts if you are serving a crowd.

MANGO-CHILI *French Toast*

I love French toast. What I don't like about it is that it takes a long time to cook, and by the time I finish cooking the last piece everything is already cold. So, I usually heat the oven and keep all the cooked toasts there. Preheating the oven gave me an idea to try making French toast there from scratch. Not the kind where pieces of bread are covered in the milky egg mixture and taste closer to bread pudding than French toast. But the actual French toast, soaked in all the goodness of milk and egg and then cooked until slightly crispy outside and firm inside. Making French toast in the oven means that you don't have to cook and flip and wait at the stove. You can just prepare everything and forget about it. So, it's a great breakfast to serve if you are entertaining. I paired my French toast with mango and spicy chili for an interesting and unique twist, but feel free to omit the pepper or even mango altogether if you prefer the classic version.

Serves 4

2 large eggs

½ cup (120 ml) milk

1 tbsp (15 ml) maple syrup, plus more for serving

½ tsp cinnamon

Pinch of salt

Oil spray

4 slices of whole wheat bread

1 mango, diced

1 tbsp (10 g) finely chopped red chili pepper

1 tsp unsalted butter, divided

Preheat the oven to 350°F (176°C). In a medium bowl, whisk together the eggs, milk, maple syrup, cinnamon and salt. Generously spray the baking sheet with oil spray. Dip each slice of bread into the egg mixture and place on the sprayed baking sheet. Evenly distribute the remaining egg mixture on top of each slice of bread.

Peel and dice the ripe mango into ½-inch (1.3-cm) pieces. In a small bowl, mix together the mango and red chili.

Spoon a quarter of the mango–chili mixture onto the center of each slice of bread. Place ¼ teaspoon of butter onto each slice of bread atop the mango mixture.

Bake in the preheated oven for 20 minutes. Serve hot with extra maple syrup.

Note: You could very easily double this recipe if you are cooking it for a larger crowd. Making the French toast in the oven means that you don't have to keep watch and cook each slice individually. Try this oven French toast with other toppings such as fresh sliced strawberries or blueberries.

Oven-Baked Maple-Sriracha *Bacon*

This bacon is everything you want bacon to be—sweet, salty, savory and spicy. It sounds and tastes fancy, like something you find at a hipster brunch place where a plate of eggs and bacon costs 25 dollars, yet it's really easy to make, and you get a lot of it for very little effort. My trick to making any bacon is cooking it in the oven on a wire rack over a sheet pan covered with foil. The hot air circulates all around the bacon, making it cook evenly on all sides without it getting soggy. The fat drips onto the foil, making cleanup really easy. Adding a maple and Sriracha mixture means that the bacon won't be crunchy-crispy; instead, it will be almost candied. There's not a lot of hot sauce, so the heat is just barely there. Feel free to add more Sriracha for a spicier treat.

Makes 8 pieces

8 pieces bacon

2 tbsp (30 ml) maple syrup

2 tbsp (30 ml) Sriracha

Preheat the oven to 400°F (204°C). Line a large, rimmed sheet pan with heavy-duty foil; it'll make the cleanup a breeze. Place a wire rack onto the foil-lined sheet pan. Arrange the bacon on the wire rack so that each piece is flat and not overlapping.

In a small bowl, mix together the maple syrup and Sriracha. Brush the maple-Sriracha mixture onto both sides of the bacon pieces. Bake in the oven for 30 to 40 minutes, depending on the thickness of the bacon and how well done you like it.

THICK OVEN *Omelet*

This thick oven omelet is a staple at Russian cafeterias in schools and daycares. It's delicious to eat warm but also great cold. Don't worry about using so much milk and cream; combined with eggs, this omelet will become really tall and spongy with a delicious caramel-colored crust. It tastes light and airy. Slice it and serve on bread for a quick morning meal.

Serves 6 to 8

1 tsp butter

6 large eggs

1 cup (240 ml) 2% milk

¼ cup (60 ml) half-and-half (10%)

¼ tsp salt

Preheat the oven to 400°F (204°C). Spread the butter all over your baking form. I use a 5 x 10-inch (13 x 25-cm) form. You can use a regular loaf pan. The narrower the pan, the fluffier and taller the omelet will turn out.

In a big bowl, whisk together the eggs, milk, cream and salt until smooth. No need to whip it, just mix it all together until well blended.

Pour the eggy mixture into the prepared pan and bake for 40 minutes. The omelet will become fluffy and tall but will deflate a little bit once out of the oven.

Note: If you'd like to increase or decrease the recipe, then the idea is that you use 50 to 60 milliliters of milk or milk/cream mixture for each egg. Try this plain version first. Later, you can add fillings like mushrooms, ham, bell peppers or cheese.

EASY OVEN-BOILED *Eggs*

I have a confession to make: I strongly dislike boiling eggs. It's not difficult and often is one of the first things a child learns to make in the kitchen, but I always have trouble. I lose track of time and over boil them. Or, horror of all horrors, I under boil them and end up with runny yolks for egg salads. The shells crack, the eggs leak, the water runs out of the pot. I avoid boiling eggs as much as possible even though boiled eggs are one of my favorite snacks.

A few years ago, I discovered the method of "boiling" eggs in the oven and was blown away by the simplicity of the method. There's no water to boil, no shells to crack. And the 30 to 40 minutes that it takes for the eggs to cook are actually more preferable to me than the traditional 10 to 15 minutes. There's not much you can do in a quarter of an hour, so you are almost certainly stuck sitting in the kitchen. Half an hour, on the other hand, means that you can do something around the house.

Serves 6

....

6 eggs   Preheat the oven to 350°F (176°C).

Place the eggs in a muffin tin: one egg into each muffin well. I like using silicone mini-muffin forms.

Bake in the oven for 30 minutes to get creamier egg yolks or 40 minutes for firmer egg yolks.

Once the eggs are baked, the shells might be covered in small brown spots. If you are using the eggs in shells for decorations, then just lightly wash the shells with a sponge to take the brown spots off.

Note: I suggest testing this method with one egg at first to figure out what timing works for your oven and your taste. Then bake a dozen or more once you know how long you need to keep the eggs in the oven to cook to your liking.

Complete One-Pan Oven Meals

I often hear from friends that cooking a complete meal after a long day at work isn't possible. It takes too much time and too much effort. And although some of the recipes in this chapter do take a long time, it's time that can be spent doing something else in the house while the oven is working its magic. And there's little more satisfying than pulling a tray out of the oven full with vegetables and protein.

Some recipes, like One-Pan Chicken and Rice with Peas (page 37) or One-Pan Lamb Loin Chops with Baby Potatoes and Carrots (page 46) require nothing else to satisfy hungry bellies. Other recipes, like Cheesy Onion Chicken Breasts with Broccoli (page 50) or Baked Haddock with Cherry Tomatoes, Capers and Lemon (page 54), may require a small helping of mashed potatoes or a bowl of rice, depending on how hungry you are. My husband needs to have some kind of grain with his meals, so a pot of rice or buckwheat is always simmering on the stove for our dinners.

Using your oven to make a complete meal requires a little bit of planning. It's not just 30 to 45 minutes of baking. You need to factor in the time that it takes to preheat your oven. My oven, for example, notoriously takes a long time to preheat, especially if the required temperature is high, like 450°F (232°C). I know that I need to turn the oven on at least half an hour but most likely 45 minutes before I want to get the food in the oven. This is why it's imperative to know your oven and its quirks, and also to have an oven thermometer. Very often, if I come home late, the first thing I do is turn on the oven to 400°F (204°C). I wash my hands and unpack groceries after. And even later, I check to see what the cooking temperature for the recipe is supposed to be.

Sheet Pan Sausages WITH SWEET POTATOES, ONION AND PEPPERS

We love sausages in my family, but there are only so many ways you can cook them. So, I rely on whatever I serve with the sausages to mix up the meals. In this particular recipe I cook Italian sausages with sweet potatoes, peppers and onions, seasoned with savory rosemary and garlic. Baking everything together allows flavors from the sausages to seep into the vegetables too. You can even chop all the ingredients a day or two early and keep them in the fridge for a very quick meal during the week.

Serves 4

1 large sweet potato

2 large bell peppers (red, yellow or orange; not green)

½ large onion

8 cloves garlic

¼ tsp garlic powder

¼ tsp salt

¼ tsp pepper

½ tsp dried rosemary

2 tbsp (30 ml) olive oil

4-6 medium Italian sausages

Spinach or mixed greens for serving

Preheat the oven to 400°F (204°C). Peel the sweet potato. Cut off the stems and remove the seeds and white ribs from the bell peppers. Cut the sweet potato and bell peppers into 1-inch (2.5-cm) pieces. Roughly chop the onion into 1-inch (2.5-cm) pieces as well.

Place all the chopped vegetables and peeled garlic onto an 11 x 17–inch (28 x 43–cm) rimmed baking sheet, sprinkle with the spices, add the olive oil and mix well so that vegetables are evenly coated in spices and oil. Spread the vegetables in a single layer, making space for the sausages in the middle.

Place the sausages onto the baking sheet between the vegetables and score them on top 5 or 6 times, about every ¾ inch (1.9 cm) or so. This will allow the juices from the sausages to easily spill onto the veggies for extra flavor.

Roast in the oven for 40 minutes or until the potatoes are soft, sausages are cooked through and an instant-read meat thermometer reads 160°F (71°C) when inserted into the sausage. Optionally, after the sausages and potatoes are cooked through, turn the oven to broil for 3 to 5 minutes to crisp up the vegetables and sausages—just be sure to watch the oven carefully so that nothing burns.

Serve with spinach or mixed greens for a full meal.

Note: You can use different kinds of sausage; just remember that some kinds are leaner and may cook faster than the potatoes, thus making the sausages a little bit dry. You can also start cooking the potatoes and add the sausages a few minutes later if they are leaner.

One-Pan Chicken AND RICE WITH PEAS

I had a really tough pregnancy with extreme fatigue. For more than half a year I barely cooked. It was difficult psychologically as I really love cooking. But during those months a mere thought of standing in the kitchen and chopping a vegetable could bring me to tears. That's when I came up with this recipe. I was looking online for some one-pot meals and most recipes, although requiring only one pot, still called for multiple steps of sautéing and precooking some ingredients. So, after a few trials I was able to create a true one-pan meal that took under five minutes to put together. I've tried this with chicken drumsticks, skinless thighs and chicken breasts also, but bone-in skin-on thighs are my favorite. The juices from the skin add delicious flavor to the rice.

Serves 4

1½ cups (315 g) basmati rice

1½ cups (250 g) frozen peas

4 tsp (8 g) seasoning mix (like Mrs. Dash no-salt seasoning), divided

½ tsp salt

8 chicken thighs (2 lbs [0.9 kg]), bone-in and skin on

3 tbsp (45 g) mayo

2½ cups (590 ml) boiling stock (chicken or vegetable)

Preheat the oven to 400°F (204°C). Add the uncooked rice and frozen peas to a 13 x 9-inch (33 x 23-cm) roasting pan (3-quart [2.8-L] capacity) with 2 teaspoons (4 g) of seasoning (I like Mrs. Dash) and the salt; mix with a spoon. Arrange the chicken thighs over the rice, skin-side-up. I always try to get as much skin facing up as possible.

In a small bowl, combine the remaining 2 teaspoons (4 g) of seasoning with mayo and brush the mixture over the chicken thighs. Pour the boiling stock over the rice around the chicken.

Bake in the oven for 45 minutes. Then broil for 2 to 3 minutes so that the skin crisps up, but be sure to watch the chicken carefully as it can burn really fast.

Note: I love this dish best with frozen peas, but I've made it with frozen corn as well as with mixed frozen vegetables. Use whatever frozen veggies you have in the freezer.

Roasted Shrimp with Feta and Broccoli

This is a really light and easy meal; it comes together in a matter of minutes. Although it's very simple, it's actually quite delicious. As with most of my recipes, if you have a bit more or a bit less broccoli, don't worry. No need to run to a store to buy an extra floret if you only have 3.5 cups (320 g). I also highly recommend using chili flakes—there's not enough to make the dish very hot, but an occasional speck of chili adds a fun dimension to the recipe.

As a side note, while I was developing this recipe for the book, I had an idea of using chunks of avocado instead of broccoli. It was my third attempt at baking with avocado, as it seems to be quite popular. Once again, I was disappointed. I still wanted to use something green, so I switched to broccoli and fell in love with this simple recipe.

Serves 2 to 4

¼ cup (10 g) chopped parsley

3 cloves garlic, minced

3 tbsp (45 ml) olive oil, divided

Zest of 1 lemon

Juice of ½ lemon

1 tsp chili flakes (optional)

Salt and pepper to taste

1 tub (7 oz [200 g]) feta, regular or light, diced into ⅓-inch (8-mm) cubes

1 lb (455 g) defrosted, cooked shrimp, peeled with tails on

4 cups (365 g) broccoli florets without stems, about 1 head

Lemon wedges for serving

Preheat the oven to 425°F (218°C). While the oven is preheating, add the parsley, garlic, 2 tablespoons (30 ml) of olive oil, lemon zest and juice to a large bowl and mix together. Add the chili flakes, if using. Season to taste with salt and pepper, though I personally don't add any extra salt as there's enough in the shrimp and feta. Add the diced feta and defrosted, well-drained shrimp to the bowl and mix well, so that the olive oil–garlic–lemon mixture covers everything.

Brush the remaining tablespoon (15 ml) of olive oil onto a baking sheet. I use an 11 x 17-inch (28 x 43-cm) pan. Transfer the feta and shrimp from the bowl onto the baking sheet and add the separated broccoli florets. Make sure that everything is evenly distributed.

Roast in the oven for 15 minutes, or until feta just begins to melt, broccoli florets are cooked and crispy and shrimp is heated through.

Serve hot with lemon wedges as a light appetizer or add a side of quinoa for a healthy and delicious meal.

Spicy Blackened Chicken Legs
WITH SWEET POTATOES AND BROCCOLI

I was going to name this recipe Jerk Chicken, but traditional jerk spices must include allspice. I've been making this marinade for many years and, although each time I keep making a mental note to buy allspice, I keep forgetting to do so. As a result, I don't feel right calling it Jerk Chicken—but it's very similar. The marinade is slightly sweet, so it caramelizes a bit in the oven and blackens as a result. The sauce mixes together with the chicken juices and is delicious over vegetables. It's not overly spicy, but if you don't like hot foods, just omit the cayenne pepper.

Serves 4

SPICY MARINADE
¼ medium onion

1 green onion

3 cloves garlic

2 tsp (1 g) dried thyme

1 tsp paprika

½ tsp smoked paprika

1 tsp cayenne pepper

½ tsp pepper

1 tsp garlic salt

¼ tsp nutmeg

2 tbsp (25 g) brown sugar

1 tbsp (15 ml) vinegar

¼ cup (60 ml) olive oil

CHICKEN AND VEGETABLES
4 chicken quarter legs, bone-in and skin-on

1 large sweet potato, peeled and chopped

1 small head broccoli, chopped

1–2 tbsp (15–30 ml) vegetable oil

Chopped green onion for serving (optional)

Preheat the oven to 450°F (232°C). While the oven is preheating, make the spicy marinade. In a small food processor, combine all the ingredients for the marinade and process until a smooth paste forms. It'll make your eyes water a little bit once you open the food processor because of all the pulverized onion. Rub the marinade all over the chicken legs and place them in the middle of the sheet pan. I use one that is 11 x 17 inches (28 x 43 cm).

Place the sheet pan with the chicken into the oven and cook for 20 minutes. While the chicken is roasting, prepare the vegetables. Peel the sweet potato and cut into 1- to 1½-inch (2.5- to 3.8-cm) pieces. Separate the broccoli into small florets and cut the broccoli stems (if using) into ½- to 1-inch (1.3- to 2.5-cm) pieces.

After 20 minutes, take the chicken out of the oven; add the sweet potatoes and broccoli around the chicken. Drizzle the veggies with the vegetable oil and return to the oven for another 30 minutes or until the internal temperature of the chicken reaches 165°F (74°C) and the potatoes are cooked through.

Serve sprinkled with green onion.

Note: If you have a larger sheet pan that will fit in the oven, feel free to increase the amount of veggies. You can also add more veggies to another sheet pan. Otherwise, I'd suggest adding rice or quinoa to make this meal more filling.

Easy Chicken Thighs in Peanut Sauce with Green Beans

When my brother-in-law got engaged, his fiancée's family invited us over for dinner. Her mom served the most delicious chicken wings. I had at least a dozen, maybe more. They were delicious and sticky and perfectly charred, and I just couldn't put my finger on what it was that made them so addicting. Finally, I asked, and it turned out that the secret ingredient was peanut butter. Those chicken wings inspired this recipe.

Serves 4

2 tbsp (30 ml) olive oil, divided

¼ cup (45 g) smooth peanut butter

2 tbsp (30 ml) lemon juice

4 tbsp (60 ml) orange juice

2 tbsp (30 ml) soy sauce

2 tbsp (30 ml) Sriracha

8 skinless, boneless chicken thighs

¾ lb (340 g) green beans

Salt and pepper to taste

Preheat the oven to 425°F (218°C). While the oven is preheating, mix 1 tablespoon (15 ml) of the olive oil with the peanut butter, lemon juice, orange juice, soy sauce and Sriracha in a bowl. I like using a small glass jug for this. It's a lot easier to mix this sauce if the peanut butter is warm. I don't have a microwave, so I put a jug with the sauce into a bowl of just boiled water to heat it up. If you have a microwave, you could heat it for 20 to 30 seconds.

Place the chicken thighs in the middle of a nonstick baking pan. I use an 11 x 17-inch (28 x 43-cm) pan. Make sure that the chicken thighs are fully flattened. Pour half the sauce over the thighs, then flip and pour the rest of the sauce, making sure that it fully covers the chicken.

Spread the green beans around the chicken thighs in one layer. Pour the remaining 1 tablespoon (15 ml) of olive oil over the green beans, season with salt and pepper to taste and lightly mix with your hands or tongs to cover them with oil and seasoning.

Roast for 30 minutes, or until the chicken thighs are cooked to 165°F (74°C) and the sauce is thickened.

Serve with rice, if desired, or double the amount of green beans and cook on a separate pan.

HOISIN MAPLE-GLAZED
Salmon with Vegetables

Hoisin sauce is my secret ingredient. I love using it in place of ketchup or BBQ sauce. It's sweet, savory, slightly smoky and has a certain umami taste to it. Add a bit of hoisin to simple rice, and suddenly you have more than just a side dish. Mix in some garlic, sesame oil, lime juice and maple syrup, and you get the most delicious sauce that gets sticky in the oven and creates a wonderful glaze for the fatty salmon. This meal is easy to prepare yet very elegant—perfect for a fancy dinner party.

Serves 4

2 cloves garlic, minced

¼ cup (60 ml) hoisin sauce

Zest of 1 lime

Juice of 1 lime

1½ tsp (7 ml) sesame oil

1 tsp maple syrup

1½ tsp (7 ml) Sriracha

1 tbsp (15 ml) soy sauce

1½ lb (680 g) salmon fillet

1-2 tsp (3-7 g) sesame seeds

1 large sweet pepper

1 small broccoli crown (about ½ lb [227 g])

¼ medium cauliflower (about ½ lb [227 g])

1 tbsp (15 ml) vegetable oil

1 chopped green onion for serving

Preheat the oven to 400°F (204°C). While the oven is preheating, prepare the hoisin glaze. In a small bowl, combine the minced garlic, hoisin sauce, lime zest and juice, sesame oil, maple syrup, Sriracha and soy sauce. Mix really well.

Line a large sheet pan with parchment paper. I use one that is 11 x 17 inches (28 x 43 cm). Cut the salmon fillet into four equal portions and arrange in the center of the baking sheet. Pour half of the hoisin glaze evenly over the fish and sprinkle with sesame seeds. Reserve the other half of the sauce.

Chop the sweet pepper into ½- to 1-inch (1.3- to 2.5-cm) pieces, and separate the broccoli and cauliflower into small florets. Arrange the vegetables around the fish, drizzle with the vegetable oil and lightly mix the veggies to coat.

Bake for 20 to 25 minutes, or until the fish is cooked to your liking. The safe internal temperature for salmon is 145°F (63°C) in the United States and 158°F (70°C) in Canada.

Serve with reserved hoisin sauce and chopped green onion.

> *Note:* I love serving this with plain basmati rice. The glaze poured over rice is absolutely delicious. You can use lemon juice and lemon zest instead of lime, but lime adds a really fun and refreshing twist to this glaze. If you choose to use lemon, a half or quarter of a lemon will be enough.

One-Pan Lamb Loin Chops
WITH BABY POTATOES AND CARROTS

Rack of lamb is a notoriously expensive cut with its delicate meat lollipops. Lamb loin chops, on the other hand, cost much less, yet they have just as much flavor. And although this meal isn't an everyday affair, it's definitely something that you could enjoy on a regular basis. I strongly suggest marinating the meat for 4 to 6 hours. Using mini potatoes and baby carrots means that there's almost no prep to the dish. Hearty and filling, it's fancy enough to serve at a dinner party but cozy enough for a family Sunday supper.

Serves 4

LAMB

3 cloves garlic, finely minced

Chopped leaves of 2 large rosemary sprigs

Leaves of 4 thyme sprigs

½ tsp salt

¼ tsp pepper

Zest of ½ lemon

Juice of ½ lemon

3 tbsp (45 ml) olive oil

8 lamb loin chops (about 2 lbs [900 g])

POTATOES AND CARROTS

1½ lbs (680 g) mini potatoes (I like using mixed potatoes as they look really pretty, but any kind would work)

¾ lb (340 g) baby carrots

Chopped leaves of ½ rosemary sprig

Leaves of 1 thyme sprig

⅛ tsp salt

1 tbsp (15 ml) olive oil

Do not preheat the oven just yet. Start with marinating the lamb loin chops. In a large bowl, combine the garlic, chopped rosemary leaves, thyme leaves, salt, pepper, lemon zest, lemon juice and olive oil. Add the lamb loin chops to the bowl and mix to make sure that the chops are covered with the marinade. Cover the bowl and refrigerate for at least 2 hours, but preferably 4 to 6 hours.

Preheat the oven to 400°F (204°C). There's no need to peel the potatoes, just wash them thoroughly. Cut the smaller potatoes in half and the larger ones in quarters. Place the potatoes into a 13 x 9-inch (33 x 23-cm) roasting pan. Scatter the baby carrots in between the potatoes. Add the chopped rosemary leaves, thyme leaves, salt and olive oil, and mix together. Cover the roasting pan tightly with foil and bake for 30 minutes.

Once the potatoes and carrots are in the oven, take the lamb loin chops out of the fridge to bring them to room temperature. After 30 minutes of baking, take the pan out of the oven and remove the foil. Place the lamb loin chops on top of the vegetables and spoon all the remaining marinade over them. Bake uncovered for 20 minutes then flip the chops. Bake for another 10 minutes if you like your lamb on the rare side, until the internal temperature of the meat reaches 145°F (63°C). Add another 5 minutes for medium lamb, until the internal temperature reaches 155°F (68°C) to 160°F (71°C). Optionally, broil for 2 to 3 minutes for a nice golden color, making sure that the meat doesn't burn.

NO-BOIL RICOTTA AND BROCCOLI
Pasta Bake

I have a lot of quirks when it comes to cooking. I don't eat celery or honey. I don't like touching raw meat. And I very strongly dislike cooking something in order to cook something else—roasting beets to make a beet salad, or boiling potatoes for shepherd's pie, or, in many cases, cooking pasta to throw together a casserole. If you can make lasagna with uncooked noodles, like in my Easy Weeknight Vegetarian Lasagna (page 80), then shouldn't you be able to make a pasta bake with dry pasta? As it turns out, you can!

This pasta bake is easy to make and requires almost no hands-on cooking, making it ideal for a weeknight meal. It tastes almost like a white lasagna with all the ricotta. Feel free to add extra vegetables to the dish—frozen peas and carrots will work wonderfully in this recipe.

Serves 4 to 6

1 small head broccoli (about 3 cups [270 g] florets)

1 mozzarella ball (9 oz [260 g]), not fresh

½ lb (227 g) dry fusilli pasta (about 2½ cups)

1 tub (10.5 oz [300 g]) smooth ricotta

¾ tsp salt

½ tsp pepper

½ tsp nutmeg

¼ tsp cayenne pepper

1½ cups (355 ml) 2% milk

½ cup (120 ml) half-and-half cream (10%)

Preheat the oven to 375°F (190°C). Separate the broccoli into florets. Cut bigger florets in half. I like separating the stalks and chopping them into smaller pieces. Grate the mozzarella cheese ball and divide in half. In a 2.5-quart (2.4-L) Dutch oven, combine the dry (uncooked) fusilli noodles, broccoli florets and stems, half of the shredded cheese and the tub of ricotta. Add all the seasonings and mix with a spoon.

Pour the milk and cream over the noodle–broccoli mixture and, using a spoon, press the dry pasta to the bottom of the Dutch oven pot, making sure that all the noodles are submerged in milk. Cover the pot with a lid and place in the oven for 50 minutes.

After 50 minutes of baking, take the pot out of the oven and mix the pasta well. Test the pasta for doneness. If it's still not fully cooked, return to the oven for another 5 minutes or until it's cooked. If the pasta is cooked, sprinkle evenly with the remaining shredded cheese, and return to the oven to melt the cheese. I like turning the broiler on at this point to get the cheese a little bit golden, but make sure to watch the stove as the cheese could go from perfectly bubbly to burnt within a few minutes.

Note: I have also made this in a ceramic, lidded pot, but I much prefer using a Dutch oven, as the texture of the dish is much better. Also, ceramic pots usually cannot be used with a broiler. If you don't have a 2.5-quart (2.4-L) Dutch oven, use an equivalent-size ovenproof pot or roasting pan and cover tightly with foil. You may need to adjust the cooking time to accommodate a different size pan.

Cheesy Onion Chicken Breasts
WITH BROCCOLI

This recipe is a variation of a classic Soviet dish called French-Style Meat. The original recipe had mushrooms, veal and béchamel sauce and was named after the 19th-century Russian ambassador to France. Like many recipes, it changed to accommodate the lack of ingredients during the Soviet era. I grew up with a variation where beef was sliced into inch-thick pieces, topped with thickly cut onions, a layer of mayo and a layer of cheese. That cheesy crust was my favorite part of the recipe; I didn't care much for the actual meat. In this recipe, I use chicken breasts, spices and very thinly sliced onions, which add moisture and textural contrast to the chicken.

Serves 4

2 tsp (1 g) onion powder

1 tsp garlic powder

2 tsp (1 g) dried parsley

¼ tsp salt

1 tsp paprika

1 cup (120 g) shredded cheddar

3 tbsp (45 g) mayo

4 cups (360 g) broccoli florets

1 tsp olive oil

¼ onion (about ⅓ cup [50 g])

4 small chicken breasts (about ½ lb [227 g] each)

Preheat the oven to 450°F (232°C). In a small bowl, mix together all the spices and set aside. In another bowl, mix the shredded cheese, mayo and 2 teaspoons (1 g) of the spices until a thick paste forms.

Spread all the broccoli florets on an 11 x 17-inch (28 x 43-cm) nonstick baking sheet on one side. Drizzle with olive oil, sprinkle with 1 teaspoon of spice mixture and mix.

Slice the onion into very thin strips. I try to make them as thin as possible: the thickness of a quarter coin or even less. Rub the rest of the spice mixture all over the chicken breasts. Place the chicken breasts onto the baking sheet next to the broccoli. Evenly divide the sliced onion and top the chicken with it. Add the mayo-cheese paste to each chicken breast on top of the onion. It will look like there's not enough cheese as it won't cover the whole breast, but spread it as much as you can over the onion and then it'll melt and cover the rest of the chicken in the oven.

Bake in the oven for 25 to 30 minutes or until the chicken reaches 160°F (71°C).

Note: Feel free to double the amount of broccoli and cook extra on a separate pan.

Pizza-Style Chicken WITH WILTED SPINACH

When I was developing this recipe, I started with just chicken breast, tomato sauce and mozzarella cheese. It wasn't going to be in this cookbook. It was just a simple, easy and—most importantly—fast dinner. After I made the chicken a few times, I realized that it tasted very similar to pizza, so I decided to add more toppings to it. The result was delicious! To round out my pizza-style dinner, I made wilted spinach in the oven. Feel free to add some diced feta to the spinach or maybe sliced bell peppers or other toppings. Just don't skip the tomatoes—you need their juices to make sure that the spinach does not get crispy and burn.

Serves 4

4 thin chicken cutlets (about 3 oz [90 g] each)

Oil spray

⅛ tsp salt, plus more to taste

⅛ tsp pepper, plus more to taste

¼ cup (60 ml) tomato sauce

8 kalamata olives, pitted and chopped

½ cup (33 g) sliced mushrooms

¾ cup (90 g) shredded mozzarella

¼ sweet onion

2 cups (227 g) cherry tomatoes

2 bags baby or regular spinach (½ lb [227 g] each bag)

2 tbsp (30 ml) olive oil

Chili flakes for serving (optional)

Preheat the oven to 425°F (218°C). Prepare two sheet pans: one larger in size, about 11 x 17 inches (28 x 43 cm), and one smaller in size, about 9 x 13 inches (23 x 33 cm). Move the middle rack in the oven to a lower position to accommodate the height of the spinach.

Spray the smaller sheet pan with a little bit of oil, and place four chicken cutlets onto it. Season with salt and pepper on both sides. Spread the tomato sauce over each chicken piece. Evenly distribute the chopped kalamata olives and sliced mushrooms over the chicken. Top with shredded mozzarella.

Slice the sweet onion thinly. Halve the smaller cherry tomatoes and quarter the larger ones. Pile the spinach onto a nonstick 11 x 17-inch (28 x 43-cm) sheet pan. Spread the sliced onion and cut-up tomatoes onto the spinach and drizzle with olive oil. The spinach will tower above the sheet pan, which is why you need a lot of space in the oven between racks.

Place the sheet pan with the pizza-style chicken onto a top rack in the oven and the sheet pan with spinach onto a middle rack. Bake for about 20 minutes or until the internal temperature of the chicken reaches 160°F (71°C). Optionally, you can also broil for 2 to 3 minutes to get a nice char on the mozzarella—just make sure that it doesn't burn.

Serve the chicken with wilted spinach, seasoned with salt and pepper to taste, and red chili flakes, if desired.

Note: Feel free to add your favorite toppings to the chicken breast. You can add sun-dried tomatoes, goat cheese, basil and so forth.

Baked Haddock WITH CHERRY TOMATOES, CAPERS AND LEMON

White fish is often not very exciting. It has a delicate flavor and may appear a bit bland. This recipe, however, is full of bright flavors and textures. There's lemon—lots of it—and sweet grape tomatoes bursting out of their thin skins; briny capers that mingle with the earthy wilted spinach; and, of course, buttery haddock with its flaked flesh. So light and summery, it reminds me of a carefree evening on a tropical vacation.

Serves 2 to 4

2 tbsp (30 g) unsalted butter

2–2½ cups (300–370 g) grape tomatoes, plus more for serving

1 lemon

1 tbsp (9 g) capers

2 cups (60 g) baby spinach, plus more for serving

2 haddock fillets (about 1¼ lbs [565 g])

Salt and pepper to taste

Preheat the oven to 425°F (218°C). Put the butter onto a quarter sheet pan (13 x 9 inches [33 x 23 cm]) and place in the oven for a few minutes to fully melt the butter. Once the butter is melted, remove the pan from the oven.

While the oven is preheating, prepare the rest of the ingredients. Halve or quarter grape tomatoes and thinly slice the lemon. Roll the sheet pan around so that the melted butter covers it all. Make sure to use your oven mitts! Scatter the tomatoes and capers onto the sheet pan, and then cover with a layer of baby spinach. Add half of the lemon slices on top of the spinach and place two haddock fillets over it. Season the fish to taste with salt and pepper, and layer the remaining lemon slices over it. I personally find that with the salt in the capers and the acidity of the lemon adding to the flavor, I don't need to add any salt to the fish.

Bake in the oven for 20 to 25 minutes, or until a safe internal temperature is reached. Safe internal temperature for the fish is 145°F (63°C) in the United States and 158°F (70°C) in Canada.

Serve with a few extra fresh grape tomatoes and spinach leaves.

Note: I love lemon and fish together, so I use a whole lemon in this recipe—both underneath the fish and on top of it. If you prefer a less acidic dish, then use only half a lemon, and arrange the lemon slices on top of the fish only.

Peameal-Wrapped Chicken Breast
STUFFED WITH BLUE CHEESE
AND ROASTED VEGETABLES

There's something about stuffed food wrapped in other food that makes it taste better. Potatoes? Yummy. Cheese-stuffed potatoes? Even better. Bacon-wrapped cheese-stuffed potatoes? Infinitely more delicious! In this recipe, I stuff the chicken breasts with blue cheese and wrap them in peameal bacon. If you can't find peameal, you can use cured, uncooked back bacon. Or, if that is also difficult to procure, just use regular bacon. The chicken breasts come out juicy and flavorful. Roasted vegetables are charred and fiery. If you prefer less spicy food, then omit the chili powder.

Serves 4

1 lb (455 g) Brussels sprouts

½ lb (227 g) baby carrots

½ lb (227 g) snap peas

¼ tsp garlic powder

¼ tsp onion powder

¼ tsp chili powder

¼ tsp pepper

½ tsp dried parsley

1–2 tbsp (15–30 ml) olive oil

4 chicken breasts (about 2 lbs [900 g])

½ cup (60 g) blue cheese, crumbled

4–8 pieces peameal bacon

Chopped fresh parsley for serving (optional)

Preheat the oven to 450°F (232°C). While the oven is preheating, prepare the Brussels sprouts. Wash them well, slice the root part off and cut them in half. I also like to discard the outer leaves as I find they often have some impurities and sand hiding in them. Cut the baby carrots in half. Add the prepared Brussels sprouts, carrots and snap peas to a large bowl.

In a small bowl, mix together all the spices. Sprinkle the spice mixture all over the vegetables, drizzle with 1 to 2 tablespoons (15 to 30 ml) of olive oil and mix well.

Cut a slit sideways in each chicken breast to create a pocket. Stuff the pockets with blue cheese. Wrap 1 or 2 slices of peameal bacon around each chicken breast. I use 1 piece for smaller chicken pieces and 2 for larger. Place the peameal bacon–wrapped chicken on the sheet pan. I use one that is 11 x 17 inches (28 x 43 cm). Spread the vegetables all around the chicken. Cook in the oven for 40 to 45 minutes, or until the chicken reaches 165°F (74°C).

Alternatively, if you prefer the vegetables to be firmer, place the chicken in the oven first and add the vegetables to the sheet pan after 15 minutes.

Remove from the oven and let sit for a couple of minutes; otherwise the hot melted cheese inside will burn. Sprinkle with chopped parsley (if using) and serve.

Note: You may also add a cup (30 g) of spinach to the chicken pockets together with the blue cheese.

EASY OVEN *Seafood Boil*

It's not a real seafood boil, as I didn't include sausages in the recipe and opted to keep it all pescatarian with the addition of salmon, but it's close enough. I like this recipe because it uses a lot of ingredients that you can keep in your freezer. Pick up some baby potatoes and sweet corn and you have delicious dinner in a matter of minutes. If you forget to defrost your seafood in advance, you can leave it in a big bowl of cold water while you are preparing the corn and potatoes. I like to lightly squeeze defrosted shrimp, and then pat it dry with paper towels.

Serves 4

3 ears corn

1 lb (455 g) small baby potatoes

1 tbsp (15 ml) olive oil

½ lb (227 g) frozen bay scallops, defrosted

¾ lb (340 g) frozen, peeled shrimp with tails on, defrosted

2 tsp (4 g) seafood seasoning, such as Old Bay Seasoning

1 tsp dried dill weed

Salt to taste, if needed

½ lb (227 g) skinless salmon fillet, either fresh or frozen and defrosted

1 tbsp (15 g) cubed butter

Lemon wedges for serving

Preheat the oven to 400°F (204°C). Cut each ear of corn into 3 to 4 pieces. Wash and halve or quarter the potatoes. Spread the corn and potatoes on a nonstick 11 x 17–inch (28 x 43–cm) sheet pan. Drizzle with the olive oil and mix well with your hands or a spatula. Bake in the oven for 25 minutes.

After 25 minutes, take the corn and potatoes out. Add the defrosted scallops and shrimp to the pan. Sprinkle evenly with Old Bay Seasoning and dill weed. I find Old Bay Seasoning salty enough so I don't add more salt, but if you prefer saltier food you could add some salt. Return to the oven for 7 minutes.

While the shrimp and scallops are cooking, cut the salmon fillet into 1- to 2-inch (2.5- to 5-cm) cubes. After 7 minutes, add the cubed salmon to the baking sheet, scattering small pieces of butter on top, and bake for another 5 to 7 minutes.

Serve with lemon.

Note: If you use a frozen salmon fillet, you can add half-defrosted salmon to the pan together with the shrimp and scallops, and they'll cook at the same time without the salmon drying out. If it's fully defrosted, it's better to add it closer to the end. I usually buy medium or small shrimp for this recipe, which are $^{41}/_{50}$ or $^{51}/_{60}$ count.

Hearty Roasted Pork Tenderloin
WITH SAUERKRAUT AND APPLES

This recipe is really simple, hearty, flavorful, delicious and quick to prepare before the pot goes in the oven to finish cooking. It's inspired by a famous Alsatian dish called *choucroute garnie*: various kinds of pork sausages, pork chops and bacon cooked together with sauerkraut, onion, garlic, juniper berries and often served with potatoes. Just like with Russian borscht, there's no set recipe for *choucroute garnie*. I love apples and pork together, and the sweetness that the fruit provides to the saltiness of the sauerkraut. You could either use apples that melt into the dish, like McIntosh, or a more firm variety that stays in pieces, like Honeycrisp. Alternatively, if apples and meat together are not to your liking, then follow the recipe but omit the apples altogether.

Serves 6

2 tbsp (30 ml) olive oil, divided

2 pork tenderloins (2-3 lbs [0.9-1.4 kg])

Salt, to taste

¼ tsp pepper

½ large onion

3 small apples

Half head garlic

1 jar (3-3 ⅓ cups [720-796 ml]) sauerkraut, drained

¼ cup (60 ml) vermouth

½ tbsp (3 g) juniper berries

Preheat the oven to 350°F (176°C). While the oven is preheating, heat 1 tablespoon (15 ml) of olive oil in a Dutch oven on medium heat. Season the pork with salt and pepper, if desired. I personally don't add any salt as I find the sauerkraut to be salty enough. Sear both tenderloins on all sides, about 3 to 4 minutes per side.

While the meat is searing, slice the onion. Core the apples and cut them into wedges. Peel the garlic and drain the sauerkraut.

Remove the pork tenderloins to a plate. Add another tablespoon (15 ml) of oil to the pan. Add the sliced onion and apples and sauté for about 5 to 7 minutes, stirring occasionally, or until the apples are softened and the onions are slightly brown. Add the vermouth to deglaze the pan and cook for a minute until it evaporates. Add the drained sauerkraut, garlic cloves and juniper berries to the pan and mix.

Nestle the seared pork tenderloins on top of the sauerkraut and transfer the pan to the oven, uncovered. Cook for about 1 hour to an hour and 15 minutes, or until the pork is cooked through, 145°F (63°C) to 160°F (71°C).

Note: Use McIntosh if you like the apples to melt into the sauerkraut or Honeycrisp if you like the apples to stay in pieces. Juniper berries add a unique, slightly peppery flavor to the dish and are used traditionally to season pork. However, they taste pretty harsh if bitten into, so remove them from the plate before eating.

Sheet Pan Shrimp, Sausage and Green Beans

Smoked sausages are one of my guilty indulgences. I survived three years at university mostly on smoked sausages and ramen noodles. Now, I allow myself to have them only a few times a year. I can't find a brand that I like that isn't too salty. In this recipe, I rely on the salt from the sausages to season the rest of the ingredients. Using cooked sausage and frozen shrimp means that this easy sheet pan meal comes together really fast. I often forget to defrost the shrimp early in the day, so I just add all of them to a bowl of cold water and they fully defrost while the oven is preheating. I then squeeze them lightly using a paper towel. For a fun twist, use smoked paprika to add even more smoky flavor to the dish.

Serves 2 to 4

¾ lb (340 g) green beans

3 cooked, smoked German sausages

1 lb (455 g) shrimp, peeled and defrosted

1 tbsp (15 ml) olive oil

½ tsp garlic powder

½ tsp onion powder

½ tsp paprika

Lemon wedges and fresh veggies for serving

Preheat the oven to 425°F (218°C). Wash and trim the ends of the green beans, if desired. Slice the smoked sausages into ¼- to ⅓-inch (6- to 8-mm) rounds. Pat the peeled shrimp dry with a paper towel.

Add the green beans and shrimp to a nonstick baking sheet. I use one that is 11 x 17 inches (28 x 43 cm), but you can use a bigger one if you'd like. Drizzle with the olive oil, add the spices and mix well. Add the sliced sausage.

Bake in the oven for 20 to 25 minutes, or until the shrimp is fully cooked. Serve with some lemon and fresh veggies.

Note: I find that the smoked sausages are really salty, so I don't add any extra salt, but you could add some if you'd like. I usually buy medium or small shrimp for this recipe, which are $^{41}/_{50}$ or $^{51}/_{60}$ count.

ONE-PAN *Fish Tacos*

There's something about having multiple plates and bowls of food on the table that makes me really happy. We have tacos or fajitas or burritos quite often for dinner. I put bowls of beans, rice, fried peppers and onions in the center of the table. I love creamy sauces and my husband prefers salsa, so bowls of those get added as well. Corn or flour tortillas get wrapped in a towel to keep warm. It seems like a lot of work, but I like the abundance of food in the bowls—and I love the choices that are in front of me. It's fun to assemble each tortilla in a different way.

In this recipe, I cook fish, peppers and onions together on one pan, making the prep a lot easier. While the fish and veggies are cooking, you have time to prepare the creamy sauce and get all your favorite taco toppings ready.

Serves 4

FISH
1 lb (455 g) cod fillet
1 tsp vegetable oil

SEASONING
¼ tsp crushed coriander seeds
¼ tsp cumin powder
½ tsp onion powder
½ tsp paprika
½ tsp garlic powder
¼ tsp citrus salt
1 tsp dried chives

VEGETABLES
1 large bell pepper
¼ red onion
1 tbsp (15 ml) vegetable oil

SAUCE
4 tbsp (60 g) sour cream
2 tbsp (30 g) mayo
2 tbsp (5 g) chopped dill
6–8 corn tortillas
Avocado, guacamole, salsa, coleslaw, cheese and so forth, for serving

Preheat the oven to 375°F (190°C). Cut the fish into 1½- to 2-inch (3.8- to 5-cm) pieces. Spread it in the center of a large sheet pan (I use 11 x 17 inches [28 x 43 cm]) and drizzle the oil over the fish. In a small mixing bowl, combine all the dry spices and sprinkle half of them over the fish.

Remove the stem, seeds and white ribs from the inside of the pepper. Slice it into ¼-inch (6-mm) strips. Slice the red onion. Scatter the sliced pepper and onion around the fish, drizzle with the vegetable oil and sprinkle with the remaining seasoning. Mix.

Bake for 15 minutes. After 15 minutes, place the corn tortillas in another small ovenproof pan and bake for 5 minutes to heat them up and finish cooking the fish. Meanwhile, prepare the sauce by mixing the sour cream, mayo and dill together.

Serve the baked fish, onions and peppers on warmed-up corn tortillas with the sour cream sauce and your favorite taco toppings, such as avocado, guacamole, salsa, coleslaw or cheese.

Note: Feel free to use your favorite taco seasoning in this recipe for an even quicker way to prepare the fish and veggies.

Sausage Bites WITH POTATOES AND CARROTS

I love roasted sausages. Edges and ends are usually my favorite—they are more charred and a little bit crispy. Cutting the sausages into little bites means that each piece will be like the ends of the sausages if they were cooked whole. I like placing them onto a wire rack and letting the hot air circulate all around, thus creating even more of those delicious, crunchy edges. The juices from the meat trickle down and flavor the carrots and potatoes that are cut so thinly they resemble chips a little bit. If you've never tried savory herb, I urge you to seek it out. It's a little bit reminiscent of rosemary but less pungent and prominent. If you can't find it at your local supermarket, omit savory altogether or use rosemary.

Serves 2

2 large potatoes (about 1¼–1½ lbs [565–680 g])

1 large carrot

½ large onion

1 tsp paprika

¼ tsp cayenne pepper

¼ tsp chili powder

¼ tsp salt

½ tsp garlic powder

2 sprigs savory herb

1 tbsp (15 ml) olive oil

4 Italian sausages

A few leaves of fresh savory for serving (optional)

Preheat the oven to 400°F (204°C). Thinly slice the potatoes, carrot and onion. You can use a food processor to make this easier and faster. In a small bowl, mix all the spices. Arrange the vegetables in one layer on a large sheet pan. I use one that is 11 x 17 inches (28 x 43 cm). Drizzle with olive oil, sprinkle with the seasonings and mix well. Scatter the savory leaves over the vegetables.

Cut each sausage into 6 to 8 pieces. It's easier to do if the sausages have been in the freezer for 10 to 15 minutes. Place a wire rack over the sheet pan with vegetables and arrange the sausage pieces on it.

Bake in the oven for 30 minutes or until the potatoes and sausages are cooked through. Optionally, broil for 2 to 3 minutes at the end to sear the sausages and add a little bit of color. Just be sure to watch the oven so that the sausages don't burn. Serve with extra fresh savory herb, if desired.

Note: For a healthier version of this dish, place the wire rack with the sausage pieces over an empty, foil-covered sheet pan. This way the fat from the sausages drains and doesn't go onto the potatoes. You may need to add extra seasoning to the vegetables if the sausages aren't cooked over them. I've tried it this way and, although yummy, I prefer everything cooked together.

Cod, Asparagus and Radicchio with Creamy Sauce

I've had radicchio many times in salads; it has a characteristic bitter taste and is very refreshing. When roasted, the bitterness gets milder, and it provides a nice contrast to the delicate cod flavor. The first time I made this recipe, I liked it so much that my husband didn't even get to try it! So the next time I cooked it, I assembled a plate and brought it to him in the home office while he was working. I cautioned him that radicchio has a bitter taste, and that it's how it was supposed to taste. I then went back into the kitchen, got myself a plate and bit into a radicchio wedge. The taste was terrible. I quickly went upstairs, only to find that my poor husband had finished the whole plate. "It was horrible," he said. I agreed. To this day, I don't know what was wrong with that radicchio—it was probably spoiled. Just remember, it's supposed to taste refreshingly bitter, nice bitter, easy bitter. Imagine the slight edge of bitterness in arugula or endive or a lemon peel. It should not taste as if you have bitten into a pill! From now on, I will taste a tiny bit of radicchio before cooking a whole head, just to make sure that it's actually edible.

Serves 2 to 4

1 small bundle (¾–1 lb [340–455 g]) asparagus

1 medium radicchio (about ½ lb [227 g])

1 lb (455 g) cod fillet

1 tsp pink peppercorns

4 tsp (20 ml) olive oil

Juice of ½ lemon

¼ tsp citrus salt

¼ cup (60 ml) half-and-half cream (10%)

1 tbsp (15 ml) grainy mustard

Salt and pepper (optional)

Lemon wedges for serving

Preheat the oven to 375°F (190°C). While the oven is preheating, prepare the vegetables. Trim the woody ends of the asparagus. I like doing it by bending each asparagus spear until it snaps and discarding the bottom part. Cut a radicchio head into quarters, and then cut each quarter into three wedges, trying to keep them intact; don't worry if they separate.

Place the prepared vegetables on a nonstick sheet pan. I use one that is 11 x 17 inches (28 x 43 cm). Mix the veggies and spread them around the edges of the pan, leaving the center empty. Cut the cod fillet into four even portions and place in the middle of the sheet pan.

Using a mortar and pestle, crush the pink peppercorns. Pour the olive oil and lemon juice over the vegetables and the fish, and then sprinkle with the citrus salt. Sprinkle the crushed pink peppercorns evenly over the cod. Mix the vegetables so that they are coated in olive oil, lemon juice and salt.

Pour the half-and-half cream into a small, oven-safe ramekin; add the grainy mustard and mix. Add salt and pepper if you like, but I personally don't add any extra seasonings. Make a little space in between the vegetables and put the ramekin there. Place the sheet pan into the oven and bake for 17 minutes.

Once baked, the sauce will get a little bit thicker but not by much. It will thicken more once it starts cooling. Pour the sauce over the fish when serving, and squeeze extra lemon juice if desired.

Hands-Off Main Dishes

I always try to incorporate some kind of vegetable into my dinner, but it doesn't have to be complicated. A handful of fresh spinach and a few cherry tomatoes make a delicious side without any effort, so you can concentrate on making your entrée and not worry about anything else. I often add chopped sweet peppers or even raw broccoli florets to the plate.

Recipes in this chapter are simple and delicious to eat with some rice or a salad. I love adding the juices from the Chicken Thighs Stuffed with Ricotta and Broccoli (page 72) to a bowl full of buckwheat. I introduced my husband to buckwheat, which is one of the most common Russian sides, and he now requests it a few times a week. If you have a chance, try it. You can make it exactly like rice and it's really delicious, nutritious and healthy.

Whenever I have family over, I often serve my Family-Style Herb and Garlic Roast Leg of Lamb (page 76). Lamb is rarely an everyday meat so it always feels special. It also requires almost no preparation. I usually make the herb and garlic butter in the morning, my husband trims the fat on the meat in the afternoon and then the oven does its work over the course of a few hours.

I love using the oven to prepare feasts. It means that I don't have to watch the pots and pans when the guests arrive, and the house fills with the aroma of roasted herbs and garlic and citrus for hours before dinner. Unlike the leg of lamb or Roast Beef with Sun-Dried Tomatoes and Kalamata Olives Tapenade (page 84), which I usually make for special occasions, Spatchcocked Chicken with Lemons and Oranges (page 79) makes a relatively frequent appearance on my dinner table. Spatchcocking it, which is just a fancy way of saying flattened or butterflied, means that the whole chicken takes less time to cook and is ready in just about an hour. And if you have a little bit over an hour to prepare a big family meal then there's nothing better than my Easy Weeknight Vegetarian Lasagna (page 80). I rely on a package of frozen spinach and a jar of my favorite pasta sauce, making the lasagna really easy to prepare.

For me, feeding a family is not about anything fancy. It's about comforting and cozy meals and the conversation that follows. It's about being surrounded with happiness and full bellies.

Chicken Thighs STUFFED WITH RICOTTA AND BROCCOLI

This is one of my go-to recipes whenever I buy chicken thighs. It's delicious, healthy, filling and is also impressive if you have company, because anything stuffed always tastes better. Ricotta has a mild taste and it's a perfect vehicle for other flavors. I add a seasoning—Mrs. Dash is my favorite—to the filling. It makes the chicken taste extra savory. Broccoli adds a fun textural contrast to the smooth ricotta. I have made these thighs with many different kinds of cheese: cheddar, mozzarella, Edam, Havarti or a mixture of a few kinds. Use whatever melty cheese you have on hand and switch them up for a slightly different taste.

The chicken thighs packed so tightly together take a bit longer to cook, but the longer they bake in the oven, the softer and more succulent they become. The juices from the chicken become almost a braising liquid and then a delicious sauce.

Serves 4

1 tub (10.5 oz [300 g]) smooth ricotta

1 large egg

1 cup (90 g) chopped broccoli florets (about 5–6 small florets)

1½ tsp (3 g) mixed seasoning, such as Mrs. Dash no-salt seasoning

½ tsp salt

1 cup (120 g) shredded cheese, such as mozzarella, cheddar, Havarti or your favorite mix, divided

Oil spray

8 skinless, boneless chicken thighs

Chopped parsley for serving

Preheat the oven to 400°F (204°C). In a medium bowl, combine the ricotta, egg, broccoli, seasonings and ½ cup (60 g) of shredded cheese. Mix well. Coat a baking dish with oil spray. I use either a pie plate that is 8 to 9 inches (20 to 23 cm) or a 10 x 7 inch (25 x 18 cm) roasting pan.

Place a big spoonful of the ricotta mixture onto the center of each flattened chicken thigh and wrap the meat around the filling. Place the stuffed chicken thighs into a prepared pan, seam-side down. The stuffed chicken thighs should fit snuggly in the pan. Depending on the size of the chicken thighs, there might be a little bit of the ricotta mixture left over. If so, spread it evenly over the chicken, and then sprinkle with the remaining ½ cup (60 g) of shredded cheese.

Bake for about 45 to 50 minutes or until the chicken is cooked through and the internal temperature of the meat reaches 160°F (71°C). Since the chicken thighs are packed tightly in the roasting pan, they take longer to cook than if they were on a baking sheet like the Easy Chicken Thighs in Peanut Sauce with Green Beans (page 42). The juices from the chicken create almost a braising liquid. I cook these thighs for an hour, as I prefer the meat a bit drier.

Serve sprinkled with chopped parsley.

Mixed Seafood WITH SUN-DRIED TOMATOES AND OLIVES

This seafood bake is really versatile. Serve it hot from the oven with big hunks of fresh bread for dipping as a delicious and hearty appetizer. Mix it with rigatoni and sprinkle with grated Parmesan for a satisfying dinner. Or spoon it over quinoa for a healthy lunch. I buy frozen seafood mix at my local Asian supermarket. There are different kinds—some with more squid rings or mussels. Some have shrimp, and some use more scallops. Find the kind you like or mix a few different kinds of seafood you prefer for a unique combination.

Serves 2 to 4

½ large onion

3 cloves garlic

¼ cup (45 g) sun-dried tomatoes in oil, lightly drained

½ cup (about 90 g) pitted Kalamata deli-style olives, approximately 15–16 olives

½ can (1¾ cups [400 ml]) diced tomatoes, with liquid; I use the no-salt version

½ tsp chili flakes

½ tsp salt

1 tbsp (15 ml) olive oil

1½-lb (680-g) package of frozen mixed seafood, defrosted and drained

Chopped parsley for serving

Preheat the oven to 375°F (190°C). Finely dice the onion; peel and thinly slice the garlic cloves. Roughly chop the sun-dried tomatoes and pit and halve the olives. Pour the diced tomatoes into a 1½- to 2-liter roasting pan. Add onion, garlic, sun-dried tomatoes, chili flakes, salt and olive oil. Mix with a spoon and place in the oven for 30 minutes. This will slightly roast the canned tomatoes and concentrate all the flavors.

After 30 minutes, add all the defrosted, drained seafood and halved olives to the tomato mixture; mix and return to the oven. Cook for another 15 to 20 minutes.

Serve sprinkled with chopped parsley.

Note: This bake is great as an appetizer with toasted bread or as a pasta sauce.

FAMILY-STYLE HERB AND GARLIC ROAST *Leg of Lamb*

When I started dabbling in cooking many years ago, I would go for the fanciest and most complicated dishes when entertaining. Now I know better! Entertaining doesn't have to be complicated, but it must be delicious, so my go-to meal whenever I have people over is an herb and garlic roasted leg of lamb. The aroma of the lamb cooking in the oven is tantalizing when people arrive. A big roast carved right at the table is always impressive. What no one knows is that this meal is really easy to prepare. I make the herb and garlic butter early in the morning and leave it on the counter. Then, a couple of hours before guests arrive, I just slather it all over the meat and let the oven do the rest.

Serves 8

4-lb (1.8-kg) boneless leg of lamb

HERB AND GARLIC BUTTER
2 tbsp (30 ml) olive oil

4 tbsp (60 g) unsalted butter, room temperature

4 cloves garlic

½ tsp salt

½ tsp pepper

¼ cup (10 g) roughly chopped parsley

4 sprigs (1 tsp [1 g]) thyme leaves

1 large sprig rosemary

Juice of ½ lime or lemon

Lemon wedges for serving

Rosemary sprigs for garnish

Take the leg of lamb out of the fridge and bring it to room temperature. Preheat the oven to 325°F (163°C). While the oven is preheating, make the herb and garlic butter. In a small food processor, combine all the ingredients for the butter and blitz together until a smooth mixture forms.

Since the leg of lamb is boneless, it will most likely come in a special net or tied up with a string. Take the string or the net off and trim the fat from the meat. I like cutting most of it off, leaving just a little bit here and there. Then slather the herb and garlic butter all over the lamb. Roll the meat into roughly the same shape as it was originally.

Place the butter-covered leg of lamb into a roasting pan and cook for about 2 hours to 2 hours and 10 minutes or until the internal temperature reaches 160°F (71°C) for medium. If you prefer the lamb to be cooked to medium rare, start checking the temperature after about 1 hour and 40 minutes. It should be 145°F (63°C).

Once cooked, let the meat rest for 5 to 8 minutes before slicing it. Serve with the juices from the pan, extra lemon wedges and rosemary sprigs for a beautiful dish presentation.

Note: This herb and garlic butter mixture works beautifully for the Addictive Garlic Cheese Toasts (page 138) as well, so feel free to double the recipe and make toasts with it.

Spatchcocked Chicken with Lemons and Oranges

Don't be scared of the word spatchcock in the name. It's only a fancy way of saying that the backbone of the chicken is removed and the bird is flattened. This technique, although daunting at first, is actually really easy—just cut the backbone out with really sharp kitchen scissors. Using flattened chicken means that it takes less time to cook in the oven. Also, there's a lot more skin exposed and it becomes wonderfully golden and crispy. Lemon, orange and onion get soft and melty; you don't even need to cut the rinds off as they get cooked. I spoon the citrus sauce over rice or quinoa.

Serves 4 to 6

1 large whole chicken (3–4 lbs [1.4–1.8 kg])

1 tbsp (15 ml) plus 1 tsp olive oil

1 large onion

1 head garlic

1 large orange

1 large lemon

2–3 sprigs thyme

1 sprig rosemary

1 tsp dried rosemary, divided

1 tsp dried thyme, divided

1 tsp salt

1 tsp pepper

Note: If you like, you can also broil the chicken for 2 to 3 minutes to get the skin crispy. Just remember that it can go from crispy to burnt in a few seconds, so make sure to watch over it carefully.

Preheat the oven to 425°F (218°C). While the oven is preheating, prepare the chicken. Place it on a cutting board breast-side down. Using kitchen shears, cut through the bones on each side of the spine—you'll end up with a long piece of chicken carcass that includes the chicken neck. Place the bones in a resealable plastic bag and freeze for a future stock if desired. Flip the chicken over, and firmly press on the breastbone to make the chicken as flat as possible.

Brush 1 tablespoon (15 ml) of olive oil over the bottom of a 13 x 9-inch (33 x 23-cm) roasting pan. Peel the onion, cut it in half, slice it into medium pieces and scatter in the pan. Add the peeled garlic to the pan. Slice the orange, without peeling it, into ⅓-inch (8-mm) rounds and place over the onion and garlic. Thinly slice the lemon and add it in between the orange slices, or on top of them. Place fresh thyme and rosemary into the center of the roasting pan. Sprinkle half the dried rosemary and half the dried thyme over the oranges and lemons.

In a small bowl, mix together the remaining dried rosemary and dried thyme. Add the salt and pepper. Rub the spice and herb mixture all over the chicken on both sides. Place the chicken skin-side up on top of the onion, garlic, orange, lemon and herbs. Try to turn the chicken legs so that as much of the skin as possible is at the top. Drizzle the remaining teaspoon of olive oil over the chicken and place in the oven for 50 to 60 minutes or until the chicken reaches a safe internal temperature. Safe internal temperature for whole cooked chicken is 165°F (74°C) in the United States and 180°F (82°C) in Canada.

Serve the chicken with the orange-lemon gravy from the pan. The fruit becomes really tender and savory.

Easy Weeknight Vegetarian *Lasagna*

For years, I have been avoiding making lasagna, as the idea of cooking long sheets of noodles and then cooling them and making sure that they don't stick together intimidated me. Also, who has time for that? Then one day I noticed a package of oven-ready lasagna noodles on a shelf at my local grocery store. I had no idea that those kinds of noodles even existed. Fast forward half a decade and this lasagna is my go-to recipe for when I have no time to spend in the kitchen. The filling comes together in a matter of minutes, assembly takes another few moments, and cleanup is just one bowl, a sieve and a few spoons. An hour later you have a delicious and flavorful meal on the table.

Serves 8 to 12

1 package (3¼ cups [500 g]) frozen spinach, defrosted

2 tubs (21 oz [600 g]) ricotta

½ tsp nutmeg

Salt, to taste

1 tsp garlic salt

¼ tsp pepper

½ tsp dried oregano

½ tsp dried thyme

¼ tsp chili powder

1 large egg

1 ball (about 9 oz [260 g]) mozzarella, not the fresh kind, shredded and divided

1 jar of your favorite tomato pasta sauce (25 oz [680 ml] or a bit more)

1 package (about ½–¾ lb [227–375 g]) oven-ready (no cook, no boil) lasagna noodles

Chili flakes for serving

Preheat the oven to 350°F (176°C). While the oven is preheating, prepare the ricotta filling. Drain the defrosted spinach using a fine mesh sieve. Press with a fork to get most of the liquid out, but don't try to make it fully dry. It's okay if there's a little bit of moisture left.

In a large bowl, mix together the drained and squeezed spinach, ricotta, all the spices, egg and half the shredded cheese. Add more salt if you prefer saltier food, but I find that there's enough salt in the sauce and cheese. Set aside.

Start assembling the lasagna. Spread a thin layer of pasta sauce at the bottom of a 13 x 9–inch (33 x 23–cm) roasting pan, about ⅓ cup (80 ml). Arrange one layer of dry oven-ready lasagna noodles on top. I am usually able to fit 5 noodles in one layer, but I have to break one of them to fit in horizontally. Spread a third of the ricotta-spinach filling on top and cover with a third of the remaining tomato sauce. Repeat 2 more times, creating 3 noodle layers. Sprinkle the rest of the shredded cheese evenly on top.

Bake for 1 hour. Serve sprinkled with red chili flakes, if desired, and your favorite salad for a complete meal.

Note: You will have about a third of the noodles left in the box; you can use them the next time you make lasagna. I can usually make 3 lasagnas out of 2 boxes of oven-ready lasagna noodles. If your jar of tomato sauce is a bit bigger, you can use a little bit more sauce—I wouldn't use less, as it would make for a drier lasagna. If you have any pulled pork leftovers or Gluten-Free Hidden Veggies Meatloaf (page 92) leftovers, then you can mix those into the sauce also.

Whole Roast Chicken Stuffed with Dry Fruit

Growing up, one of my favorite meals was chicken with prunes. My mom would stick prunes under the skin of drumsticks or thighs and bake until the skin was golden brown and the prunes were soft and sticky. The combination of sweet and salty is still my favorite. This roasted chicken stuffed with dried fruit is inspired by my childhood favorite, and if you like fruit and meat together, I am sure it will become your favorite too. The fruit becomes sweet and savory, permeated with chicken juices and seasoned with garlic and lemon. The onion underneath the chicken turns sweet and jammy and is a great accompaniment to the succulent meat.

Serves 6 to 8

¼ cup (30 g) pecan halves

¼ cup (38 g) pitted prunes

¼ cup (38 g) dried apricots

¼ cup (22 g [about 3 rings]) dried apple, roughly chopped

8 large cloves garlic

1 lemon

½ large onion

½–¾ tsp salt

1 large whole chicken (3–4 lbs [1.4–1.8 kg])

1 tbsp (15 ml) olive oil

Preheat the oven to 425°F (218°C). While the oven is preheating, prepare the fruit stuffing mixture. In a small bowl, combine the pecan halves, prunes and dried apricots. Add the dried apples and garlic cloves to the bowl. Cut the lemon into 8 pieces, and add 4 of them to the fruit mixture.

Slice half the onion into thick strips and scatter at the bottom of a roasting pan. Arrange the other 4 pieces of lemon between the onions. Generously salt the chicken outside and inside. Spoon the fruit mixture into the chicken cavity and pack firmly. It might seem like there's too much stuffing, but just keep packing it in and it'll fit. Tie the chicken legs together with baker's twine, and place the chicken over the sliced onion and lemon. Brush the top of the chicken with the olive oil to encourage a delicious, crispy skin.

Roast in the oven for 1½ hours or until the chicken is beautifully golden brown and its internal temperature reaches 165°F (74°C) for the United States or 180°F (82°C) for Canada. I like basting the chicken with its juices twice after an hour in the oven.

Let the chicken rest for 5 to 8 minutes before carving. Serve with the onions and juices from the pan, a bit of dry fruit stuffing and your favorite side. I love this chicken with Alan's Favorite Roast Potatoes (page 126).

Roast Beef with Sun-Dried Tomatoes and Kalamata Olives Tapenade

Roast beef in my family is something we eat relatively often. It's something I make on the weekends just for us and also for company. Tapenade sounds fancy but it is really just a mixture of sun-dried tomatoes, Kalamata olives, garlic and lemon juice finely minced together in a food processor. A big hunk of beef is then covered with this salty and tangy paste and roasted for a few hours. The flavors meld together and create the most beautiful and savory sauce that goes perfectly with the meat. I like steaks to be pink inside, but I like roast beef to be fully cooked. I then slice it thinly when cool and make delicious roast beef sandwiches the next day.

Serves 4 to 6

¼ cup (45 g) sun-dried tomatoes in oil, lightly drained

¼ cup (45 g) pitted deli-style Kalamata olives

1 clove garlic

2 tbsp (30 ml) olive oil

Juice of ¼ lemon

2 lbs (900 g) sirloin tip oven roast or eye round roast

Preheat the oven to 450°F (232°C). While the oven is preheating, add the tomatoes, olives, garlic, oil and lemon juice to a food processor and mince until an almost smooth paste forms. I don't fully drain the sun-dried tomatoes when making tapenade. Just pick them up with a fork from the jar and lightly shake; if there's some oil left on the tomatoes, that's fine also.

Place the beef into a roasting pan and rub the tapenade all over the roast, even at the bottom. I usually use a spoon to get the tapenade onto the meat without touching it. This way the tapenade is not contaminated and the bowl can be licked clean—it's that good!

Place the roasting pan into the oven and cook for 10 minutes. This high-heat cooking quickly sears the meat. Reduce the heat to 325°F (163°C), and cook for about 2 hours for a medium-well roast. Always check the internal temperature of the meat with a thermometer. Medium-well is 160°F (71°C). If you prefer your roast beef more rare, then 145°F (63°C) internal temperature is also food-safe, it will take about 1 hour and 45 minutes to reach that temperature. Make sure that you know your oven, as some ovens cook food faster than others. Start checking internal temperature every 15 minutes after 1½ hours.

Note: You can also use a top or bottom round roast cut.

Baked Trout WITH FRESH SALSA AND CHEESE TWO WAYS

This is my best friend Clara's recipe. One day, over breakfast, we were talking about food, as many of our conversations tend to go that route, and she told me how back in university she used to make salmon with salsa and cheese. I was intrigued since I don't usually think of fish and cheese together. Clara didn't have any specific measurements, so I experimented a bit and was really surprised at how easy and delectable it was. I love using two different salsas for some variety, and also because my husband doesn't like fruit salsa. With only three ingredients, the dish comes together really easily: spread salsa over fish, cover fish with melty cheese, bake and enjoy. Fresh salsa works better for this recipe; you can find it at your grocery store usually near the salads, but you can also make your own. Feel free to use your favorite homemade salsa as well. I bet pineapple would go excellent with the fish.

Serves 2 to 4

2 rainbow trout fillets (½–¾ lb [227–340 g] each)

¼ cup (60 ml) fresh tomato salsa, drained

¼ cup (60 ml) fresh mango salsa

3 slices mozzarella cheese or about ½–¾ cup (60–90 g) shredded mozzarella

Preheat the oven to 350°F (176°C). Cover a baking sheet large enough to fit two rainbow trout fillets with parchment paper. Place the fish fillets onto the prepared baking sheet.

Drain the tomato salsa in a fine-mesh sieve. This is an optional step but highly recommended. Undrained salsa will be a bit messy on the baking sheet, as the tomato juices will run. Spread the drained salsa over one of the fillets. Mango salsa does not usually need to be drained, but if there's liquid then drain it too and spread it over the other fish fillet.

Cover each fillet with 1½ slices of cheese or, if you are using shredded mozzarella, evenly split it between two fillets.

Bake for 15 minutes, or until the fish reaches a safe internal temperature. The safe internal temperature for trout is 145°F (63°C) in the United States and 158°F (70°C) in Canada. Broil for 2 to 3 minutes to brown the cheese a little bit. When broiling, make sure to watch the oven carefully as the food often goes from beautifully browned to burned in a matter of seconds.

Note: Fresh salsa is usually found in the refrigerator section at your local grocery store either near the cheeses or near the salads and herbs, and sometimes in the area where pre-chopped vegetables are sold.

Easy Fish AND BOILED EGGS PIE

Fish pies are very popular in Russia. The most traditional fish pie is called *coulibiac*, or *kulebyaka*, and it usually has layers of salmon, buckwheat and fried mushrooms separated by thin crepes and all wrapped in flaky pastry. Over the decades of communism, empty store shelves and the ingenuity of Russian people, the recipe changed. Sun-shaped crepes were removed to save time and effort. Buckwheat and mushrooms were so rare that it was a shame to add them to the pie. And golden, buttery pastry that took hours to prepare was replaced by a quick, cake-like batter.

Eggs, mayo and buttermilk (or kefir if you'd like to keep this recipe even more Russian) create the base for the batter. It will look thick and a bit strange, but I guarantee you it will spread and puff up in the oven, encompassing the fish and egg filling. Eat this pie cold or warm as a snack, or serve with salad and a glass of white wine for a delicious lunch.

Serves 6 to 8

BATTER

3 large eggs

¾ cup (175 ml) buttermilk (or kefir)

¼ cup (60 g) mayo

1 tbsp (15 ml) Dijon mustard

¼ tsp dried dill

¼ tsp salt

½ tsp sugar (optional)

¼ tsp cayenne

1 cup (125 g) all-purpose flour

¾ tsp baking powder

FILLING

¾ lb (340 g) skinless salmon fillet (about 1 lb [455 g] with skin)

3 large hard-boiled eggs, peeled (Easy Oven-Boiled Eggs, page 31)

⅓ cup (12–15 g) chopped dill

¼ tsp citrus salt

Preheat the oven to 350°F (176°C). Make the batter. In a medium bowl, combine all the ingredients except for the flour and baking powder. Whisk until smooth. Add the flour and baking powder and mix until just combined and the flour disappears. Do not overmix.

To make the fish filling, chop the salmon fillet into ¾- to 1-inch (2- to 2.5-cm) pieces. Then finely chop the hard-boiled eggs. In a medium bowl, mix together the chopped eggs, salmon, dill and citrus salt.

Line an 8 x 8–inch (20 x 20–cm) square baking dish with the parchment paper. Pour about one-third of the batter into the prepared pan and spread thinly. Cover with the fish and egg filling. Pour the remaining batter and spread over the fish filling. It will seem like there's not enough batter, but that's how it's supposed to look. Just spread it around as well as you can. It'll expand and puff up while baking.

Bake for 45 minutes. If the pie isn't golden brown after 45 minutes, then brush lightly with oil and broil for just a little bit, maybe 1 to 2 minutes. Just make sure to watch the oven like a hawk to prevent the pie from burning. Serve warm or cold with salad.

Note: You can use this batter for many different kinds of savory pies. Try chopped cooked chicken and fried onion, sautéed cabbage with chopped boiled eggs or cooked ground beef and peppers.

DELICIOUS MINI DILL *Meatballs*

I love baking meatballs in the oven as I can make them in large quantities without much effort. Imagine pan-frying 50 meatballs on the stove: all the splattering oil and turning the meatballs on all sides, not to mention that they won't fit into one pan and need to be cooked in batches. Shaping the walnut-sized meatballs and promptly sliding them into the oven makes life so much easier.

Use these dill meatballs for the traditional spaghetti and meatballs, add them to sandwiches, serve on toothpicks as an appetizer or add to soups.

Dill is one of those herbs that for some reason isn't really popular in North America. I grew up eating dill almost daily. My mom always has dill in her fridge and adds it to almost everything she makes. In my family, we even add a bunch of dill to a vegetable platter and eat it like a carrot stick or a cherry tomato. It adds a unique vibrancy to the meatballs and makes them taste bright, light and fresh. If you don't like the flavor of dill, feel free to use flat leaf parsley instead.

Makes around 50 meatballs

1 lb (455 g) lean ground beef

1 lb (455 g) extra lean ground chicken

1 large egg

⅓ cup (40 g) panko breadcrumbs

½ cup (20 g) finely chopped dill

1 tbsp (6 g) seasoning, such as Mrs. Dash no-salt seasoning

½ tsp garlic salt or to taste

Preheat the oven to 400°F (204°C). Line a big sheet pan with parchment paper.

In a large bowl, thoroughly combine all the ingredients until they are mixed really well. Shape the ground meat into walnut-sized meatballs and arrange on the prepared sheet pan so that they don't touch each other.

Bake for 25 to 30 minutes or until the internal temperature of the meatballs is at least 160°F (71°C). It'll be around 180°F (82°C) after 30 minutes, and the meatballs will still be juicy.

Note: I personally like drier meatballs, so I often bake them for 40 to 45 minutes. You may use any combination of ground meat, but if you use extra-lean chicken or turkey only, the meatballs will be drier than if lean beef or pork is added into the mix.

GLUTEN-FREE HIDDEN VEGGIES *Meatloaf*

I love the idea of adding vegetables to ground meat, thus stretching an expensive ingredient, adding some bulk and also nutrients. What I don't like is pieces of carrots mixed into smooth, ground-meat texture. Processing all the vegetables together into almost a paste hides them and doesn't affect the texture of the meatloaf. Potato and onion also add moisture to ground turkey, so there's no need to add an egg or breadcrumbs.

Serves 6 to 8

1 large carrot (⅓ lb [150 g]), peeled

½ large yellow onion (⅓ lb [150 g]), peeled

1 medium potato (⅓ lb [150 g]), peeled

1 tsp garlic powder

1 tsp Italian seasoning

1 tsp salt

½ tsp pepper

2 lbs (900 g) ground turkey

¼ cup (60 ml) plus 1 tbsp (15 ml) your favorite BBQ sauce (I prefer the smoky kind)

Preheat the oven to 450°F (232°C). While the oven is preheating, peel and roughly chop the carrot, onion and potato. Place the vegetables in a food processor and mince for 1 to 2 minutes until the mixture is almost smooth. Add all the spices and mix for a few seconds to incorporate them.

Put the ground turkey into a large bowl, add the vegetable mixture, a ¼ cup (60 ml) of BBQ sauce and mix really well with a spatula or your hands.

Transfer the meat mixture into an 8-inch (20-cm), round cake form (be sure to use a one-piece form, not a springform, or the juices will leak out of it) or an 8 x 8-inch (20 x 20-cm), square baking form and flatten it. Put the baking form with the meatloaf into the oven to cook.

After 30 minutes, brush the remaining 1 tablespoon (15 ml) of BBQ sauce on the meatloaf and return to the oven for 1 more hour, or until the internal temperature of the meatloaf reaches 165°F (74°C).

Once the meatloaf is cooked, it'll have a lot of meat juices around the edges. Let the meatloaf stand for 5 to 10 minutes, and the liquid will absorb back into the meatloaf.

Notes: Don't worry if each of the vegetables doesn't weigh exactly ⅓ pound (150 g). The idea is that carrot, onion and potato combined should weigh about 1 pound (454 g), so you end up with 1 pound (454 g) of vegetables and 2 pounds (900 g) of ground turkey.

SPICED BACON-WRAPPED *Pork Roast*

I don't make pork roasts too often as they tend to dry out quickly. I prefer making pork chops or schnitzel (like my Oven-Fried Schnitzel Sandwiches, page 100). One of my favorite tricks for juicy pork is an addition of bacon on top. The juices from the bacon add much-needed moisture to the meat and the result is soft and succulent. This pork is great served with Alan's Favorite Roast Potatoes (page 126) when hot or sliced thin and used for delicious sandwiches.

Pork rib roast isn't the most common cut of meat, but try finding it if you can. It's a little bit fattier than tenderloin, but not by much, and it has a more distinct and meatier taste.

Serves 4

SPICE RUB
2 tsp (4 g) garlic powder

¾ tsp cayenne pepper

1 tsp paprika

¼ tsp salt

½ tsp pepper

1 tsp dried thyme

PORK ROAST
1½ lbs (680 g) boneless pork rib roast

1 tsp vegetable oil for the pan (optional)

4 slices bacon

Preheat the oven to 375°F (190°C). While the oven is preheating, make the spice rub. In a small bowl combine all the spices and mix well. Rub the spice mixture all over the pork roast.

Brush the vegetable oil onto a roasting pan, if using. Place the pork roast on the pan and wrap it with bacon. Roast in the oven for about 1 hour or until the internal temperature of the roast reaches 145 to 150°F (63 to 66°C). Cover with foil and rest for 10 minutes.

Note: If you can't find boneless pork rib roast, you can use a pork tenderloin. You may need to roast it for less than an hour since this cut of meat is thinner. Start checking for doneness after about 45 minutes.

Cocoa-Rubbed Pork Back Ribs with *Chocolate BBQ Sauce*

A few years ago, I hosted a chocolate dinner party, and every course had either cocoa or chocolate in it. For the main course we had cocoa-rubbed ribs with chocolate BBQ sauce. Cocoa powder in the rub acts mostly as a vehicle for other seasonings and flavors. Instead of increasing the amount of spices to cover all the ribs and making the rub overly intense, I use cocoa powder. Chocolate chips in the BBQ sauce add a touch of sweetness to the sauce, but not enough to make the meat taste like a dessert.

Serves 2 to 4

Cocoa Rub

1 tbsp (7 g) cocoa powder

1½ tsp (7 g) brown sugar

1 tsp onion powder

1 tsp garlic powder

¼ tsp pepper

½ tsp chili powder

½ tsp paprika

¼ tsp salt

1 large rack pork back ribs (about 2 lbs [900 g])

BBQ Sauce

¼ cup (60 ml) your favorite BBQ sauce (I like using the smoky kind)

¼ cup (45 g) semi-sweet chocolate chips

¼ tsp chili powder

¼ tsp smoked paprika

Chopped green onion for serving

Preheat the oven to 300°F (149°C). While the oven is preheating, make the cocoa rub by combining all the dry ingredients in a small bowl and whisking them together. I like doubling the ingredients and then saving half of the rub in a container for the future.

Remove the thin membrane from the back of the ribs. It sounds intimidating but it's actually quite easy. Slide a sharp tip of a knife under the membrane and turn it slightly to loosen the white skin, then slide your finger in the resulting pocket and slowly start moving it along the ribs under the membrane. You should be able to grasp the end of the membrane and just pull it off.

Place the ribs on a large piece of heavy-duty foil and rub all over with the cocoa spice rub. Wrap tightly with the foil and transfer the wrapped rack of ribs onto a baking sheet, seam-side up. Cook in the oven for 3 to 4 hours.

After the ribs are done cooking, heat the BBQ sauce in a small pot over medium heat. Add the chocolate chips and let them melt into the sauce, stirring constantly. Add the chili powder and smoked paprika and mix. Remove the ribs from the foil and place on the baking sheet. Be careful not to spill the fat from the foil, as it can get messy. Brush some of the chocolate BBQ sauce all over the ribs and return to the oven. Broil for about 3 to 5 minutes, watching the meat constantly to make sure that it doesn't burn.

Serve with chopped green onion and leftover chocolate BBQ sauce.

Simple Soups, Salads and Sandwiches

My husband's favorite food is soup, lentil soup to be precise. It's so easy—just sauté a little bit of onion, add the lentils and vegetable stock and cook until everything is soft. I like adding a few squeezes of lemon juice, and my husband always adds chili powder. His eyes light up whenever I make any kind of soup and he can eat two, three or sometimes even four servings easily. This is exactly the reason why I don't make soup often. It's a bit disconcerting seeing a huge pot of soup disappear in a matter of minutes when it should have lasted for at least a few days. The soups in this chapter can easily be doubled and tripled if you have someone in your household that loves soup as much as my husband does. Just roast a few extra vegetables and add a bit more stock for a bigger pot.

Oven-Fried Schnitzel Sandwiches (page 100) take some effort to make with all the breading of the pork, but they are so worth it—crispy, crunchy and without all the extra oil of deep frying. But if you'd like a really satisfying sandwich without much fuss, then you must make the Turkey-Swiss Sliders with Cranberry Sauce (page 107). I guarantee you won't be able to stop at just one.

Unlike my hubby, who loves salads with more leaves and lettuces than anything else, I prefer bulkier and more filling salads. My Roasted Tomatoes and Chicken Panzanella Salad (page 104) is delicious, healthy and really easy—just roast chicken breast, tomatoes and bread in the oven and mix with some fresh veggies! And almost nothing can beat thick, salty, melty pieces of halloumi cheese served atop a mountain of roasted vegetables (Salad with Roasted Vegetables and Halloumi Cheese, page 103). It's a hefty salad that will satisfy both vegetarian and meat eaters.

Oven-Fried Schnitzel *Sandwiches*

Whenever I make schnitzels, I put them on a wire rack over a baking sheet in the oven to keep crispy. Yet, by the time I finish making all the schnitzels, I am usually exhausted. I'm tired from watching over the pan with hot oil, and I'm hot from the heat of the oven. This is why I came up with the idea of making delicious schnitzels in the oven. No need to guard yourself from the splattering of oil, no need to make food in batches. Everything is cooked together in the oven at the same time. Mind you, the schnitzels will never be as crispy as the ones made on the stove, but they will be a lot healthier and the panko breading still gives them a nice crisp coating.

Serves 4 to 6

6 boneless thin pork loin chops (about 1-1¼ lbs [455–565 g])

2 large eggs

2 tbsp (30 ml) milk

1 cup (50 g) panko bread crumbs

1 tsp (7 g) garlic salt

4 tsp (2 g) dried parsley

¼ cup (30 g) all-purpose flour

1 tsp pepper

1 tbsp (15 ml) vegetable oil

Oil spray

Buns, lettuce, sliced tomatoes, mustard or sauce for serving

Lemon wedges for serving (optional)

¼ cup (55 g) mayo

¼ cup (60 g) plain yogurt

1 tbsp (15 g) Dijon mustard

Preheat the oven to 400°F (204°C). While the oven is preheating, pound the pork chops as thin as possible, about ¼-inch (6-mm) thickness or just a bit under it.

Prepare three shallow and wide bowls. Mix the eggs and milk until smooth in the first bowl. Mix the panko bread crumbs, garlic salt and parsley in the second bowl. Mix the our and pepper in the third bowl.

Once the oven is preheated, brush the vegetable oil onto an 11 x 17-inch (28 x 43-cm) baking sheet, preferably nonstick. Use a bit more oil if yours doesn't have a nonstick coating. Place the baking sheet with the oil into the oven to preheat for about 5 to 7 minutes.

Bread the pork chops. Take each pork chop and dip it into the flour mixture, making sure the pork chop is fully drenched in it. Shake off the excess flour and dip the pork chop into the egg mixture, covering it on both sides. Finally, dip the egg-covered pork chop into the panko breadcrumb mixture, pressing the breadcrumbs onto both sides of the pork chop. Repeat with the rest of the chops.

Working quickly, remove the sheet pan from the oven, lay the breaded pork chops onto it and generously spray the tops of the chops with the oil spray. Bake for 10 minutes.

After 10 minutes, flip the pork chops and generously spray with oil on the other side. Bake for another 10 minutes or until the internal temperature of the schnitzels reaches 145°F (63°C) for the United States or 160°F (71°C) for Canada.

Once the schnitzels are cooked, broil for about 2 to 3 minutes, making sure that the schnitzels don't burn. You could broil on both sides or just one.

For the creamy sauce, mix together the mayo, plain yogurt and Dijon mustard.

Assemble the sandwiches by spreading mustard or sauce on the bottom half of the bun. Add cooked schnitzel, sliced tomatoes and lettuce. Squeeze some lemon juice over the schnitzels if desired.

Salad WITH ROASTED VEGETABLES AND HALLOUMI CHEESE

Hide the eggplant is a game that I often play in the kitchen. My husband doesn't like eggplant and I do, so I try to find ways to sneak it into my recipes without him noticing it. My husband adores salads, and this one is not an exception. I usually serve it all mixed for him and hide the eggplant this way. It visually disappears in the midst of golden halloumi, charred peppers and sweet and smoky tomatoes. The salad is a beautiful medley of colors, flavors and textures: chewy cheese, slightly crunchy onion, soft eggplant. I personally love eggplant and cilantro together so if I make this salad for myself only, I use cilantro to make pesto instead of parsley.

Serves 2 to 4

SALAD
2 Chinese eggplants (½ lb [227 g])

1 large sweet pepper

3 Roma tomatoes

½ large onion

1 head garlic, peeled

2 tbsp (30 ml) olive oil

½ lb (227 g) halloumi cheese

4 cups (120 g) spinach

PESTO DRESSING
1 cup (40 g) roughly chopped parsley

½ cup (60 g) walnuts

2 tbsp (30 ml) olive oil

2 tbsp (30 ml) water

Juice of ¼ lemon

¼ tsp salt, or more to taste

Preheat the oven to 400°F (204°C). Line a large, rimmed baking sheet with parchment paper. Cut the stem part off the eggplants and slice into ¼- to ⅓-inch (6- to 8-mm) rounds. Halve the pepper and remove the stem, seeds and white ribs from the inside. Halve and deseed the tomatoes. Slice the onion into medium pieces. Peel and separate the head of garlic into cloves. Arrange all the prepared vegetables on the baking sheet, brush them with the olive oil, and bake for 30 to 40 minutes depending on how cooked you like your vegetables.

While the vegetables are roasting, slice the halloumi into 6 to 8 ¼-inch (15- to 21-cm) slices. After 30 to 40 minutes in the oven, flip the vegetables and move them around a bit to make space for the cheese. Add the halloumi slices to the sheet pan and return to the oven for another 5 minutes. Then broil for 2 to 3 minutes until the cheese turns slightly golden. Make sure to really watch the oven as the cheese can go from golden to burnt in just a few seconds.

Meanwhile, make the parsley pesto. In a small food processor, combine all the ingredients for the pesto and process until smooth. If you prefer thinner pesto, then add a little bit of extra water or olive oil.

Once the vegetables are cooked, remove from the oven. Slice the tomatoes and peppers into thin strips. Optionally, you could remove the skin from the tomatoes and peppers if you'd like. Fill a large bowl with spinach and add all the vegetables and broiled halloumi cheese. Mix in the pesto and serve with fresh bread.

ROASTED TOMATOES AND CHICKEN
Panzanella Salad

Traditional Italian panzanella salad is made with stale bread and raw tomatoes. In my version, I rely on fresh ciabatta that is toasted in the oven together with the chicken and cherry tomatoes. Juicy chicken breast, crunchy croutons, sweet and bursting-from-their-skin tomatoes: together they make up the most delicious, filling and healthy dinner salad. The dish is brilliant in its simplicity. It works great in the summer when the tomatoes are at their finest, but it's also perfect in the winter as the high roasting temperature concentrates the sugars in the tomatoes, making them sweeter and juicier.

Serves 4

PANZANELLA

1–2 tbsp (15–30 ml) olive oil, divided

2 chicken breasts (about ½ lb [227 g] each)

¼ tsp salt

2 tsp (5 g) Italian seasoning

1 lb (455 g) cherry tomatoes

1 small ciabatta roll (¼ lb [115 g])

¼ red onion

1 large English cucumber

DRESSING

¼ cup (60 ml) olive oil

1 tbsp (15 ml) Dijon mustard

1 tbsp (15 ml) balsamic vinegar

Salt to taste

Preheat the oven to 450°F (232°C). Brush 1 teaspoon of olive oil onto a large baking sheet, preferably nonstick. I use one that is 11 x 17 inches (28 x 43 cm). Brush the chicken breasts with 2 teaspoons (10 ml) of olive oil, season with the salt and Italian seasoning on both sides and put them on the baking sheet. Add the cherry tomatoes to the sheet pan. Place in the oven for 15 minutes.

While the chicken is roasting, slice the ciabatta into 1- to 1½-inch (2.5- to 3.8-cm) pieces. After the initial 15 minutes of roasting, add the ciabatta pieces to the baking sheet, brush 2 to 4 teaspoons (10 to 20 ml) of olive oil over the ciabatta pieces, and return to the oven. Bake for another 15 minutes, or until the chicken is cooked through and the internal temperature of the meat reaches 160°F (71°C).

Meanwhile, make the balsamic dressing. In a small bowl, combine the olive oil, Dijon mustard, balsamic vinegar and salt, and whisk until smooth. Alternatively, add all the ingredients into a small, lidded mason jar and shake. Roughly chop the red onion and the cucumber.

To serve, dice the chicken and mix together with the chopped red onion, cucumber, toasted ciabatta and roasted tomatoes. Dress with the balsamic dressing.

Turkey-Swiss Sliders WITH CRANBERRY SAUCE

With these easy sliders, you can have the familiar flavors of Thanksgiving dinner any time of the year. Mini rolls—whether brioche, potato or Hawaiian—turn a humble sandwich into a unique and exciting meal. Try finding rolls that come in one big rectangular slab instead of individual buns—it will make assembling the sliders a lot easier. After the rolls are baked, it's fun pulling them apart and watching the melted cheese stretch in between the sandwiches. For a different twist on this recipe, use various kinds of cheeses and deli meats.

Makes 12 sliders

12 brioche mini rolls (or mini dinner rolls or Hawaiian rolls)

1 tbsp (15 g) mayo

1 tbsp (15 ml) Dijon mustard

10 slices oven roasted turkey breast (6-oz [175-g] package)

⅓ cup (80 g) cranberry sauce (homemade or store bought)

1 tbsp (15 ml) horseradish

6 big slices of your favorite Swiss cheese (about 5 oz [150 g])

1 tbsp (15 g) butter

½ tsp garlic powder

1 tbsp (2½ g) chopped parsley, plus more for serving

Preheat the oven to 375°F (190°C). I love using brioche buns for the sliders, as they are a bit sweeter, but you can also use regular unsweetened rolls. The main thing is that they should come as one big slab and not as individual rolls. Slice the tops off the mini rolls.

Transfer the bottom part of the rolls onto a baking sheet or roasting pan big enough to fit the rolls. In a small bowl, mix together the mayo and Dijon mustard and spread the mixture on the bottom part of the rolls. Layer the turkey slices overlapping slightly on the rolls.

In a small bowl, mix the cranberry sauce with the horseradish and spread the mixture over the turkey. Add the Swiss cheese, and cover with the top part of the rolls.

In another small bowl, melt the butter and add the garlic powder and parsley. Brush the butter mixture over the rolls. Bake for 12 to 15 minutes to heat the bread through and melt the cheese. Sprinkle with more parsley for serving.

Note: My husband notoriously doesn't like sweet and savory combinations, so I usually only spread the cranberry and horseradish mixture on half of the rolls. If you are also not a fan of sweet and savory, omit the cranberry sauce all together. If you like the look of the ruby red layer of sauce in the sandwich but not the sweetness that comes with it, try finding a beet-flavored horseradish—it tastes the same as the regular kind but looks gorgeous and festive.

CREAMY ROASTED TOMATO AND *Pepper Soup*

Tomato soups weren't popular in Russia when I was growing up. In fact, the first time I even tried tomato soup was some time during my university years. Right away I understood the fascination with this simple dish paired with a grilled cheese sandwich. In my recipe, I use both tomatoes and sweet bell peppers to add some depth of flavor. Juicy, vine-ripened, roasted tomatoes melt in your mouth and, combined with charred peppers and smooth cream, turn into a delectable, comforting and cozy soup. It's delicious with a grilled cheese sandwich or my crunchy Addictive Garlic Cheese Toasts (page 138).

Serves 2 to 4

2 large, red sweet peppers

6 vine tomatoes (about 1½ lb [680 g])

¼ tsp sea salt, or more to taste

1 tbsp (15 ml) olive oil

½ cup (120 ml) half-and-half cream (10%)

Preheat the oven to 400°F (204°C). Cut the peppers in half, then remove the seeds and white ribs from the inside. Cut the tomatoes in half, and cut out the green stem part. Place the vegetables cut-side up on a roasting pan in a single layer. Sprinkle the salt over them, and flip them over so that they are skin-side up now. Drizzle with the olive oil and bake for 1 hour.

Once baked, remove the skins from the tomatoes and peppers. I find that I can use tongs to do it right away, as the skin usually just peels off easily. Alternatively, you can place the vegetables into a bowl and cover tightly with plastic wrap to let them steam for 10 to 15 minutes, and the skin will be easier to peel.

Transfer the peeled vegetables and all the juices from the roasting pan into a blender. Then add the cream, blending until smooth and creamy. Add more salt if desired.

This soup tastes amazing with the Addictive Garlic Cheese Toasts (page 138).

CREAMY ROASTED EGGPLANT *Soup*

I grew up eating eggplant, and it is still a favorite of mine. My husband, however, isn't really a fan of this vegetable. This soup is one of a few recipes where he loves the flavor. The smoked paprika in the soup complements the charred vegetables. The garlic adds sweetness and cayenne pepper makes it just a little bit spicy. It's really easy to make, as you just roast the vegetables and then puree them with a bit of stock. You can even roast the veggies a day before, and blend everything and heat it up when you plan to serve the soup.

Serves 2 to 4

1 large tomato, or two medium (about ¾ lb [340 g])

1 large Italian eggplant (about 1 lb [455 g])

1 large bell pepper: red, yellow or orange but not green (about ½ lb [227 g])

5 large cloves garlic

1 tbsp (15 ml) olive oil

2 cups (480 ml) vegetable stock

½ cup (120 ml) half-and-half cream (10%) (optional: use more stock instead for a vegan version)

2 tsp (5 g) smoked paprika

½ tsp salt, or more to taste

½ tsp garlic powder

½ tsp cayenne pepper (optional)

Crackers for serving

Parsley or cilantro for serving

Preheat the oven to 400°F (204°C). Prepare the vegetables by slicing them in half lengthwise. Remove the stems from the tomato and eggplant. Remove the seeds and white ribs from the inside of the pepper.

Place all the vegetables in a roasting pan in one layer, cut-side up, and scatter the garlic in between the vegetables. Pour the olive oil over the vegetables and lightly rub all over.

Roast the veggies in the oven for 1 hour and 20 minutes or until the vegetables are fully cooked and soft, flipping them halfway. When turning the vegetables, cover the garlic cloves with halves of the pepper to prevent the garlic from burning.

No need to peel the vegetables, but if you'd like the soup to have a smoother consistency, you can easily take the skin off the vegetables after they are roasted.

Once the vegetables are cooked, roughly chop them and place in a blender with the stock. Blend until smooth.

Pour the soup into a pot and warm gently to your desired heat level. Add the cream and spices; mix. Serve with crackers and cilantro or parsley.

Note: For thinner soup, add a little bit more stock.

Mini Chicken *Meatball Subs*

These mini chicken meatball subs are a great appetizer, or even lunch if served with salad. The recipe can easily be doubled if you are making them for a crowd. Don't be scared of the pumpkin puree in the meatball mixture. You cannot taste the pumpkin, yet it adds fiber, vitamins and moisture. It binds the mixture together instead of an egg. And if you are looking for more ways to use up pumpkin puree, try my Simple Apricot and Plum Cobbler (page 162).

Serves 8

Oil spray for the pan (optional)

1 lb (455 g) ground chicken

2 green onions, finely chopped

¼ tsp salt

¼ tsp pepper

¼ cup (60 g) pumpkin puree

1 cup (120 g) shredded mozzarella, divided

8 small dinner rolls (about 2½ inches [6.4 cm] in diameter)

¼ cup (60 ml) pasta sauce

More pasta sauce and green onion for serving

Preheat the oven to 425°F (218°C). Either cover a 9 x 13-inch (23 x 33-cm) sheet pan with parchment paper or spray with cooking oil. In a big bowl, combine the ground chicken, chopped green onion (both green and white parts), salt, pepper, pumpkin puree and ½ cup (60 g) of shredded mozzarella cheese. Mix well.

Cut out the centers of the dinner rolls and press with a spoon inside to make little bowls. Divide the meatball mixture evenly between 8 bread bowls. Spread the pasta sauce over the meatball mixture and sprinkle with the rest of the mozzarella cheese. Bake for 30 minutes or until the internal temperature of the meatballs reaches 165°F (74°C). Serve sprinkled with a little bit more green onion and some extra pasta sauce for dipping.

Note: I like using brioche rolls as they are a bit sweet and make a delicious contrast with the savory meatballs, but any small rolls will work.

Caramelized Onion Oven *Soup*

There's something comforting about the smell of frying onions. The sizzle of the oil when they hit the hot pan, the aroma of caramelizing sugars, the magic of a mountain of white half circles reducing into a handful of sweet and jammy onions: I love everything about making an onion soup except the amount of work it takes. Cooking onions until they are soft and the color of dark chocolate isn't difficult, but you need time, patience, a glass of wine and a lot of stirring.

It's no wonder that I tried making caramelized onions in the oven. I didn't really expect it to work and was very surprised when it did. Caramelizing onions in the oven takes a little bit longer than doing it on the stove, but there's almost no hands-on cooking time. It makes this soup an ideal recipe for a lazy weekend.

Serves 4

5 large onions (1½ lbs [680 g], 8 cups [1.9 L] sliced)

2 tbsp (30 ml) olive oil

1 tbsp (15 g) butter

¼ cup (60 ml) vermouth (optional)

8 cups (1.9 L) broth (vegetable or chicken/meat-based)

Salt and pepper to taste

Fresh thyme for serving

Preheat the oven to 400°F (204°C). Very thinly slice the onions. I use a food processor for this; it takes only a few minutes and no tears. Add the olive oil to a large Dutch oven, fill it with the sliced onions, put the lid on and place in the oven.

Cook for 1½ hours, stirring every 20 minutes. After 1½ hours, the onions will be deeply brown, sweet and jammy. They will reduce to just over a cup in volume. Carefully remove the pot from the oven, add the butter and vermouth (if using) and mix with a spatula until the butter melts. Add the broth, cover with the lid and return to the oven for another hour.

Season with salt and pepper to taste, add some fresh thyme leaves and serve. This soup goes great with the Addictive Garlic Cheese Toasts (page 138). Alternatively, you can make it into a traditional French onion soup by topping each bowl with a piece of toast and grated cheese and baking until the cheese melts before serving.

Easy Sides

Whenever I make dinner, I concentrate on the main course, and by the time it's cooking in the oven and I finish cleaning up, I realize that I have nothing to serve with it. So usually, I end up cooking some kind of grain that I find in the cupboards. However, if I plan a little bit ahead, I love making something fun, healthy and delicious to serve with meals.

Potatoes are my all-time favorite side. Any kind of potatoes would suffice, although I am very partial to simple mashed potatoes. In fact, whenever someone asks me what my favorite food is, my answer is always mashed potatoes. Strangely enough, I don't make mashed potatoes often. Alan's Favorite Roast Potatoes (page 126), on the other hand, are a very frequent occurrence in my kitchen. The times I have woken up in the middle of the night from the smell of a pot of lentil soup simmering on the stove or the aroma of these roasting potatoes that my husband decided to have as a midnight snack are too many to count. And although lentil soup wouldn't be my food of choice at two in the morning, I can see how making it is quite easy. Roast potatoes, on the other hand, take some effort and a few hours to prepare. So you know they are really good if someone makes them in the middle of the night!

There are times when I make a double batch of the Roasted Summer Vegetables (page 121) or Roasted Brussels Sprouts with Apples and Bacon (page 122) or Roasted Cauliflower, Sweet Potato and Garlic Mash (page 130) and have them as a main course or a quick lunch. Add a side of toasted pitas or simple Applesauce Cornbread (page 125), and I am in healthy, delicious food heaven. By the way, if you've never tried Roasted Carrots and Radishes (page 118), you are in for a treat! Radishes' sharp bite is mellowed from the heat, and they become slightly buttery. Make sure to try roasting them next summer when they are sold fresh, just pulled out of the earth, at your local farmers' market.

ROASTED CARROTS AND *Radishes*

The concept of roasting radishes may seem a bit strange, but give it a try. I promise, you won't be disappointed! Cooking radishes in the oven mellows them out a little bit. They turn from sharp and nippy to mild and a little bit buttery, yet still spicy. Paired with sweet carrots and drizzled with lemon juice and thyme, this recipe tastes like spring—bright and beautiful. Technically, you don't have to use bunches of radishes and carrots with greens still attached. Individual radishes and baby carrots will suffice, but that little bit of greenery adds a whimsical touch to the dish. And we eat with our eyes first, don't we?

Serves 2 to 4

1 bunch radishes with greens

1 bunch young carrots with greens

1 tbsp (15 ml) olive oil

¼ tsp salt

¼ tsp pepper

3 or 4 sprigs thyme

Juice of ¼ or ½ lemon

More lemon and fresh thyme for serving

Preheat the oven to 450°F (232°C). Wash the radishes and cut the greens off, leaving just a little bit of the stalk. Cut the bottom roots off. Leave small radishes whole, but cut the medium ones into halves and the large ones into quarters.

Wash and scrub the young carrots really well since they won't be peeled. Cut the greens off, leaving a little bit of the stalk. Cut the longer carrots in half and leave the shorter carrots whole.

Place the prepared radishes and carrots onto a small baking dish in one layer. Add the olive oil, salt, pepper, thyme leaves and lemon juice. Mix well.

Bake for 20 to 30 minutes depending on how soft you like your vegetables. Serve with an extra squeeze of lemon juice and a few fresh thyme leaves on top.

Note: Growing up, I always ate radishes slathered with butter and sprinkled with salt. I thought it was a Russian thing, but years later I started seeing those three simple ingredients together in recipes from all over the world. If you like radishes and butter together, then add a little bit of butter to the olive oil before cooking. Or add some butter once the radishes and carrots are cooked and let it melt into the vegetables.

ROASTED *Summer Vegetables*

I am not the biggest zucchini and squash fan, but I love the vegetables in this recipe. I think it's because this whole dish looks extremely beautiful and I feel excited eating it. It's bright and colorful and simple. The high roasting temperature ensures the vegetables cook quickly and their natural sugars concentrate. Thyme is one of my favorite herbs to use with vegetables; it adds a delicious and barely perceptible depth of flavor while not overpowering the natural taste of the produce. This recipe is the perfect way to celebrate summer bounty.

Serves 4

1 medium zucchini (½ lb [227 g])

2 small yellow summer squashes (½ lb [227 g])

1 large sweet bell pepper (½ lb [227 g])

½ head Romanesco—if you can't find it use either cauliflower or broccoli

10 pearl onions

1 tbsp (15 ml) olive oil

3–4 sprigs thyme plus more for serving

½ tsp salt

Pepper, to taste

Preheat the oven to 425°F (218°C). While the oven is preheating, prepare the vegetables. Slice the zucchini and squash into ¼-inch (6-mm) circles. Chop the pepper into ½-inch (1.3-cm) pieces. Roughly separate and chop the Romanesco (or cauliflower or broccoli, if using) into small florets. Peel and halve the larger pearl onions and leave the smaller ones whole.

Add all the vegetables to a sheet pan (I use one that is 11 x 17 inches [28 x 43 cm]), drizzle with the olive oil, sprinkle with the thyme leaves, season with the salt and pepper, and mix. Roast in the oven for 15 minutes if you like crunchier vegetables. I prefer my vegetables to be a bit softer, so after 15 minutes, I mix everything with a spoon and roast for another 10 minutes.

Serve sprinkled with a few fresh thyme leaves.

Note: Pearl onions are notoriously difficult to peel. Supposedly you can boil them for a minute or so to soften the skin. I've never tried it. I usually chop a little bit off each end of the onion and then peel the skin and top layer off.

Roasted Brussels Sprouts WITH APPLES AND BACON

Whether you are serving this side for Thanksgiving dinner or just as a treat for a Sunday supper, you won't be disappointed. Sweet apples and salty bacon balance each other and go really well with roasted and slightly crispy Brussels sprouts. Brussels sprouts usually take a little bit of time to wash, peel and cut. You can prepare them a day in advance and store in the fridge. Then the next day, it will only take a couple of minutes to chop an apple and the bacon and throw this whole dish together.

Serves 4

2 lbs (900 kg) Brussels sprouts

1 large Gala apple (about ½ lb [227 g])

3–4 slices bacon

1 tbsp (15 ml) olive oil

Sea salt and chili flakes for serving

Preheat the oven to 400°F (204°C). While the oven is preheating, prepare the Brussels sprouts. Wash them well, cut the root part off and cut them in half. I also like to discard the outer leaves, as I find they often have some impurities and dirt hiding in them. Scatter the prepared Brussels sprouts onto a sheet pan. I use a nonstick one that is 11 x 17 inches (28 x 43 cm).

Core the apple and roughly chop into ½-inch (1.3-cm) pieces. Cut the bacon slices into 1- to 1½-inch (2.5- to 5-cm) pieces. Add the apples and bacon to the pan with the olive oil. I prefer not to add salt once everything is cooked, as there's enough salt in the bacon and bacon juices; if you prefer saltier vegetables, add a bit of seasoning before baking. Mix everything well with a spatula, and bake in the oven for 30 to 40 minutes if you like the Brussels sprouts to be a bit crunchy. I prefer the vegetables to be softer, so I cook for 40 to 50 minutes.

Serve sprinkled with salt and chili flakes.

APPLESAUCE *Cornbread*

Cornbread is one of the foods that I forget about for months. Then when I see a recipe online or in a magazine, I get inspired—and a little bit obsessed—and usually make it once a week for a month before forgetting about it again. A lot of recipes for cornbread call for cups of oil or sticks of butter, and although those recipes taste amazing, I prefer to make mine a little bit healthier.

This particular cornbread is simple; the recipe can be used as a base for many different variations. I've made it with jalapeños, corn kernels, extra cheese. Feel free to add cayenne pepper or smoked paprika. You can even use half blue cornmeal and make this into a marbled cornbread by slightly mixing two different colored batters together.

I love using applesauce in baking to replace some of the oil. It adds much-needed liquid and a slight sweetness to the batter. For a fun variation, feel free to replace the applesauce with pumpkin puree.

Serves 8

2 tbsp (30 ml) vegetable oil

½ cup (120 ml) unsweetened applesauce

3 large eggs

½ cup (120 ml) buttermilk

1 cup (170 g) yellow cornmeal

1 cup (125 g) all-purpose flour

½ tsp salt

1 tsp baking powder

1 cup (120 g) shredded cheddar

½ diced jalapeño (optional)

½ cup (70 g) drained canned corn (optional)

Preheat the oven to 375°F (190°C). Line an 8 x 8-inch (20 x 20-cm) square baking dish with parchment paper. In a large bowl, combine the vegetable oil, applesauce, eggs and buttermilk. Whisk together until smooth. Add the cornmeal, flour, salt and baking powder; mix until combined. Add the cheese, jalapeños (if using), drained canned corn (if using), and mix.

Spoon the mixture into the prepared baking dish and bake for 40 minutes, or until baked through and a toothpick inserted in the middle comes out clean.

Note: I use applesauce in this recipe instead of mostly oil. It adds moisture as well as a slight sweetness. However, the bread will get a bit drier the next day, because there's not a lot of oil in it; so for softer cornbread, it's better to eat it within a couple of days. It will keep in an airtight container in the fridge for 5 days.

ALAN'S FAVORITE *Roast Potatoes*

These potatoes are my husband's recipe. He usually doesn't measure the spices, yet the potatoes turn out exactly the same every time. After years of making them, he just knows how much seasoning to add. We usually double this recipe, or sometimes triple it, and eat the potatoes as a snack, side and even breakfast. Over the years, there were more times than I could count when I woke up in the middle of the night to the smell of these potatoes, because Alan got hungry and wanted a snack. These roast potatoes have a nice spicy edge to them. If you prefer less spicy food, then reduce the amount of chili powder—but they will be very different.

Serves 4

2 lbs (900 g) potatoes

½ tbsp (7 ml) vegetable oil

½ tbsp (7 ml) olive oil

½ tsp pepper

¼ plus ⅛ tsp chili powder

¼ tsp garlic salt

Preheat the oven to 400°F (204°C). There's no need to peel the potatoes, just wash and scrub them really well. Cut the potatoes into 1½- to 2-inch (3.8- to 5-cm) chunks. Place them into a big bowl, pour both oils over them and add all the seasoning. Cover the bowl with either a lid or a plate, and shake vigorously so that the potatoes are evenly covered in oil and spices.

Transfer all the potatoes into a 13 x 9-inch (33 x 23-cm) roasting pan and place in the oven. Bake for 40 minutes and then flip the potatoes. They may stick to the pan in places; that's to be expected. Bake for another 50 minutes (1½ hours altogether), until the potatoes are cooked through and are golden brown. Serve as a side or as a snack with ketchup.

Note: My husband prefers these potatoes to be crispier, so we often leave them in the oven for almost 2 hours.

Easy Scalloped Potatoes AND Carrots

This dish isn't an everyday side with the vegetables cooked in cream and cheese. It's a little bit lighter and healthier than your traditional scalloped potatoes, yet it's utterly delicious, creamy and cheesy. If you have a few extra minutes, a lot of patience and guests to impress, then you can even arrange the potatoes and carrots into beautiful stacks, alternating vegetables and placing them in neat rows in the roasting pan. I've done that once. I won't do it again as I was almost crying by the end of the stacking experience half an hour later. But it was gorgeous! This recipe is super easy if you have a food processor, as it does most of the work.

Serves 4

2 lbs (900 g) potatoes (5 medium)

1 lb (455 g) carrots (3 large)

1 tsp unsalted butter

1½ cups (180 g) shredded mozzarella, divided

1½ cups (355 ml) half-and-half cream (10%)

½ tsp pepper

¾ tsp salt

¾ tsp garlic powder

¾ tsp nutmeg

¼ tsp cayenne pepper

4 sprigs thyme (1 tsp), plus more for serving

Preheat the oven to 400°F (204°C). Either using a mandoline, a food processor or by hand, thinly slice the potatoes and carrots. Butter a small, 2-liter roasting pan. I use a metal pan that is 10 x 7 inches (25 x 18 cm) that can be used with a broiler. Mix the potatoes and carrots, spreading half of them onto the prepared pan. Sprinkle ½ cup (60 g) of mozzarella cheese, and arrange the rest of the potatoes and carrots on top.

In a medium bowl, whisk together the cream and all the seasonings and spices. Pour the cream mixture evenly over the potatoes and carrots, and sprinkle the rest of the mozzarella cheese on top. Cover the baking dish tightly with foil, and bake for about 1 hour and 20 minutes or until the potatoes and carrots are fully cooked. Remove the foil and broil for 2 to 3 minutes, making sure to watch the oven as the cheese may go from bubbly and golden to burnt in just a few seconds.

Let stand for a few minutes to cool a bit and serve sprinkled with fresh thyme leaves.

Note: This is one of those recipes where you need to know your oven. Mine always takes a long time to cook potatoes. Yours might be done after an hour, or they may need a full 1½ hours, so check for doneness before serving.

ROASTED CAULIFLOWER, SWEET POTATO AND GARLIC *Mash*

This delicate, orange-colored mash looks absolutely gorgeous on a plate. It's slightly sweet, creamy and has a very distinct roasted garlic flavor. Add generous pieces of butter and watch them melt into golden pools over the mash. Don't try making it without a food processor. Even though the cauliflower is cooked until it's very soft, it still cannot be mashed well by hand. I tried making this recipe with a potato masher and ended up with a bowl of chunky half-mixed vegetables. You want the texture to be silky smooth—and that requires a food processor.

Serves 4

1 large sweet potato

1 medium head cauliflower

1 head garlic

¼ cup (60 ml) cream (10%, 18% or 35%)

½ tsp salt, or more to taste

Pepper to taste

Butter for serving

Preheat the oven to 400°F (204°C). Wash the sweet potato and cauliflower. Pierce the sweet potato with a fork all over and tightly wrap in foil. Cut out the stem from the head of cauliflower and discard it. Wrap the cauliflower in a big piece of foil. Chop the top end off the head of garlic; then wrap the whole garlic head in foil. Place all three foil parcels onto a large roasting pan, and bake for 2 hours until the vegetables are very soft.

Once cooked, very carefully—so as not to burn yourself—scoop out the sweet potato from its skin and place into a food processor. Squeeze out the garlic cloves from the skin and add to the food processor as well. Be careful not to burn yourself. Add the cauliflower, cream, salt and pepper. Process the mixture until smooth, stopping and scraping the sides a few times. Serve with a few dabs of butter and extra salt and pepper, to taste.

Note: Squeezing the hot garlic requires some finesse. The garlic skin cools pretty fast, but the actual garlic flesh stays piping hot for a while. I always try squeezing the skin without touching the inside, although I do burn myself a little bit. You can cool everything if you'd like before making the mash, and then gently heat on the stove in a pot.

One Pan, Many Nibbles

If I could, I would only eat appetizers! I love appetizers, snacks or nibbles. It must be a Russian thing. Growing up, no celebration was without a table covered in copious plates and bowls filled with everything from mayo-laden salads to pickles, smoked fish, deviled eggs, pâtés, vegetables, breads and cheeses. The first time my husband went to a Russian restaurant, he was impressed: The table was covered in plates and plates of food. It never occurred to me to let him know that it was just the first course. He ate, and ate, and then ate some more. He tried everything within reach, and an hour later he was full and completely satisfied. That's when the second course arrived.

Even now, whenever I host a party, I spend most of my time preparing various nibbles. Roasted Fennel with Cheese (page 134) is a staple—so easy to prepare, and always delicious. Tarts (try my Beet and Goat Cheese Tart on page 142 or Pear, Blue Cheese and Walnut Puff Pastry Tart on page 145) are a cinch to make using frozen puff pastry or filo dough, and they look impressive served cut into squares or on top of a simple salad.

The day after the party, I usually forgo any regular meals in favor of huge platters of assorted nibbles: some bread and a few different kinds of cheeses for breakfast; Popovers with Vegetables (page 141) and a healthier version of spinach and artichoke dip (Cottage Cheese Spinach and Artichoke Baked Dip, page 137) for lunch; a delicious charcuterie platter filled with various salamis; and my homemade Pastrami-Style Chicken Breast (page 146) for dinner. And, of course, no trip to the kitchen is complete without sneaking a piece or two of the Addictive Garlic Cheese Toasts (page 138).

Roasted Fennel WITH CHEESE

Many years ago, my then fiancé and I found a small Italian restaurant next to a jewelry place where we were getting my engagement ring and our wedding bands made. It took a few visits to talk about the design, approve the moulds, change the sizing. And each time we visited that shop we had dinner at the restaurant next door. One of the items they always had on their menu was an antipasto platter that often included fennel with Parmigiano-Reggiano. After I had it a few times, I finally asked for the recipe and, surprisingly, the chef shared it with me. That dish included fennel, cheese and butter—a lot of butter! I think it was half a teaspoon of butter for each slice. I started making the recipe, modifying it and only placing pea-sized drops of butter onto the vegetables, but it still was messy. In this recipe, I adapted the original idea, reduced the amount of butter and made the whole process a lot easier. I also added some breadcrumbs to make the topping a bit crunchy.

Serves 6 to 8

½ cup (90 g) grated Parmigiano-Reggiano

¼ cup (30 g) panko breadcrumbs

1 tbsp (15 g) cold butter

¼ tsp garlic powder

¼ tsp paprika, plus more for serving

Salt, to taste

1 large fennel bulb

Preheat the oven to 400°F (204°C). Measure out ½ cup (60 g) of Parmigiano-Reggiano and add to a small food processor. Pulse until you get coarse crumbs. Add the panko breadcrumbs, butter, garlic powder, paprika and salt. Pulse for about 1 minute, or until everything is mixed together into a fine crumb mixture.

Prepare one large, and possibly one smaller, baking sheet and cover with parchment paper. Depending on how thin you are able to slice the fennel, you might need to use both sheet pans. Trim the fennel bulb. Cut the top and the bottom root part off. Place the fennel root-side down onto a cutting board, and slice the bulb into very thin pieces, about the width of a quarter coin. Place each slice onto a prepared baking sheet. Most likely, since fennel has layers, slices will separate. Don't worry about it—just combine pieces together on the sheet pan. I often just place stray pieces into small piles at the end.

Evenly divide the cheese–crumb mixture between the fennel slices. Start with about ½ teaspoon to make sure that each slice of fennel has some crumb topping. Add more topping to larger pieces.

Bake for 25 minutes. If you are using two sheet pans, then switch them around midway. Serve with an extra sprinkling of paprika if desired.

> *Note:* I usually process a big chunk of Parmesan (Parmigiano-Reggiano) in a food processor until it's a fine to medium crumb, measure out ½ cup (60 g) for this recipe, and store the rest in an airtight container in the fridge to use later.

Cottage Cheese, Spinach and Artichoke *Baked Dip*

Dips are one of my favorite appetizers. What's not to love? You take something crunchy and dip it into something melty—it's the perfect combination! This cottage cheese, spinach and artichoke dip is a play on the classic flavors with a twist. This dip is actually healthy, so you can have seconds and thirds since it's made with delicious cottage cheese that is blitzed in a food processor. Add some thawed spinach and drained artichokes, and the dip comes together in a matter of minutes, making it a perfect party or even weeknight dinner appetizer.

Makes about 2 cups

1 tub (17½ oz [500 g]) cottage cheese, 1% or more

⅓ cup (60 g) thawed and fully drained chopped spinach (about 100 g while it's still frozen)

½ cup (85 g) artichokes in oil, drained

1 tbsp (15 g) mayo

1 tsp garlic powder

¼ tsp salt or more to taste

¼ tsp cayenne pepper

2 sprigs thyme

½ cup (60 g) shredded cheese: cheddar, mozzarella or Monterey Jack

Preheat the oven to 400°F (204°C). While the oven is preheating, pour the cottage cheese into a fine mesh sieve and shake a few times over a sink. You'll see that some whey will come out. You don't want to fully drain the cottage cheese, just shake it 5 to 8 times. Add the cottage cheese to a food processor and pulse until smooth, about 30 to 45 seconds. Add the spinach and artichokes and pulse a few times until the artichokes are chopped into bite-size pieces. Add the mayo, spices and thyme leaves and mix.

Pour the cottage cheese mixture into an ovenproof 5 x 5-inch (12½ x 12½-cm) dish and sprinkle with the shredded cheese.

Place the dish with the dip on a baking sheet to catch accidental spillovers and bake in the oven for 15 minutes or until the dip is heated through and the cheese is melted and bubbly. Serve with pita, chips or crackers. Sprinkle with fresh thyme for an extra-savory flavor.

The dip is quite light since it uses cottage cheese as a base. For a more indulgent treat, add a little bit of extra shredded cheese into the dip mixture. And if you are really pressed for time, you don't even need to bake it—just serve right from the food processor!

Note: I thaw spinach in a fine mesh sieve and press with a fork to make sure it's very well drained and almost dry. You also don't technically need to drain the cottage cheese. If you know that you have a big crowd coming and there will be no dip left at the end of the night, then I wouldn't even bother draining the cottage cheese. Removing some of the whey helps the dip stay a bit thicker if you have leftovers. I've made this dip with both undrained and drained cottage cheese.

ADDICTIVE GARLIC *Cheese Toasts*

Believe it or not, I've never made traditional garlic bread: the one you get in a basket at Italian restaurants, soft and buttery with a golden crust. A couple of years ago my husband asked me to make garlic bread, and I thought I'd wing it. I bought ciabatta rolls, made garlic butter and put the bread in the oven. Half an hour later I had a tray of the biggest croutons I've ever seen. And although my first attempt at garlic bread didn't yield the results we were expecting, those crunchy garlic ciabattas were delicious. Two days later I tried again. This time I sliced a baguette into rounds and toasted them with the garlic butter, adding some cheese to a few of them. Since then, I haven't even tried making the soft garlic bread, as we actually prefer these golden, round garlicky cheese toasts. They are delicious as an appetizer or a snack and go perfectly with soup, such as Creamy Roasted Tomato and Pepper Soup (page 108) or Caramelized Onion Oven Soup (page 115).

Makes 30 to 35 pieces

4 tbsp (60 g) unsalted butter, room temperature

2 tbsp (30 ml) olive oil

3 large cloves garlic, minced

1 tsp garlic powder

¾ tsp garlic salt

½ tsp onion powder

½ tsp dried thyme

1 tsp dried parsley

1 baguette

About ½ lb (227 g) of cheese, any kind: Monterey Jack, cheddar, mozzarella, Gouda, etc.

Preheat the oven to 375°F (190°C). Prepare the garlic butter by mixing the butter, olive oil, garlic and the rest of the herbs and spices in a small bowl until a smooth paste forms. Alternatively, use a small food processor to prepare the garlic butter.

Cover a large baking sheet with parchment paper. Slice the baguette into ⅓-inch (0.8-cm) slices. You'll get about 30 to 35 pieces. Spread a little bit of the garlic butter onto each piece of bread and place on the baking sheet butter-side up. Top with the cheese. I don't usually shred the cheese for the toasts, I just slice it thinly and arrange it on top of the bread. I also like to leave a few pieces of bread without the cheese.

Bake them in the oven for 12 to 15 minutes, or until the cheese is melted and the bread is starting to crisp up and turn golden. Once the cheese toasts are done, they will be really melty for the first few minutes, but then the cheese will harden. If you can resist eating all of them right away, they'll last up to 2 days at room temperature, covered.

These toasts are great with soup or as a snack with a glass of cold beer.

Note: Adding olive oil to the mixture means that even though the garlic butter will be solid in the fridge, it'll get very soft and spreadable within a few minutes of being on the table.

Popovers WITH VEGETABLES

If you want to impress your guests, serve these popovers with dinner or as nibbles with cocktails. The batter for these gorgeous little puffs comes together easily in a blender—there's no whisking or mixing by hand. The addition of chopped vegetables is unique and adds a fun texture and flavor to the otherwise simple bread rolls. You could chop all the veggies a day or two ahead and keep them in an airtight container to make the preparation of the popovers even easier and faster. I love using the popovers as a base for sandwiches or to soak up some delicious juices from roasts. Try them with Family-Style Herb and Garlic Roast Leg of Lamb (page 76) or with Spatchcocked Chicken with Lemons and Oranges (page 79).

Makes 6 popovers

2 large eggs

1 cup (240 ml) milk

1 cup (125 g) all-purpose flour

½ tsp salt

½ tsp sugar (optional)

Oil spray

3 tbsp (30 g) very finely chopped onion

¼ medium sweet bell pepper, very finely chopped, about ⅓ cup (55 g)

2 medium broccoli florets, tops only, finely chopped, about ½ cup (45 g)

1 tbsp (15 g) butter

Preheat the oven to 450°F (232°C). While the oven is preheating, prepare the batter. Place the eggs, milk, flour, salt and sugar (if using) into a blender and blitz for about 45 to 60 seconds until a very smooth batter forms. Scrape down the sides to make sure that all the flour gets incorporated, and blend for another few seconds.

Prepare a 6-cup standard-size (medium) metal muffin tin. Generously spray oil into each of the 6 muffin wells. Distribute all the chopped vegetables evenly between each of the muffin cups. Veggies should be about halfway up the tin. Split the butter evenly between each muffin tin.

Place the muffin pan into the oven for 5 to 6 minutes so that the vegetables are slightly softened and cook a little bit and the butter melts.

Take the muffin pan out of the oven and, working really quickly, pour the batter into each of the muffin cups. It should fill each cup almost completely to the edge. Immediately return the pan to the oven and bake for about 30 to 35 minutes (I bake them for 33 minutes in my oven) without opening the oven. If you know that your oven tends to run hot, then the popovers may be done sooner. They are done when they have risen significantly above the muffin pan, are golden brown and sound hollow if you knock on them.

Once the popovers are cooked, take the muffin pan out of the oven and pierce each popover with a sharp knife on the side to let the hot steam escape. Let the popovers cool in the pan for a few minutes before taking them out of the pan. They will have a thick center and a hollow pocket inside, and the veggies will have been distributed along the sides of the popovers.

Note: You can easily double the recipe and make 12 popovers, but you might need to increase baking time by about 5 minutes. The popovers are better eaten the same day, but they can keep in the fridge for 1 to 2 days, though the texture will change a little bit.

BEET AND GOAT CHEESE *Tart*

Most of the recipes for beet tarts require using precooked beets. And although beets aren't particularly difficult to cook—just wrap them tightly in foil and bake in the oven for a couple of hours—it seems like an unnecessary step when they have to go back in the oven on top of paper-thin filo pastry. Beets notoriously take a long time to cook, but slicing them thin means they will soften in just half an hour. In this tart, beautiful golden and ruby sweet beets are paired with creamy and salty goat cheese and sprinkled with earthy thyme. This appetizer is delicious warm or cold, and it's perfect with some slightly sweet and bubbly rosé wine.

Serves 8

3 medium beets, preferably in two colors (about 12–14 oz [350–400 g])

6 filo sheets

¼ cup (60 ml) vegetable oil

3–4 sprigs thyme (1 tsp fresh thyme leaves)

½ cup (60 g) crumbled goat cheese

Sea salt to taste

Preheat the oven to 375°F (190°C). Wash and peel the beets. Using a mandoline or a food processor, thinly slice the beets. You can also do it by hand if you like. Cover a large baking sheet with parchment paper. I use one that is 11 x 17 inches (28 x 43 cm).

Place two sheets of the filo pastry onto a baking sheet and brush with a little bit of oil. Cover with another two sheets of filo pastry and brush with more oil. Add the last two sheets of filo on top, and roll the edges a little bit on each side to create a border. The size of the filo crust with the edges rolled will be around 11 x 13 inches (28 x 33 cm). Arrange the beets on top of the crust and brush with the remaining oil. Scatter the fresh thyme leaves and crumbled goat cheese over the beets.

Bake for about 30 to 35 minutes or until the edges of the filo get golden brown and the thinly sliced beets are soft and cooked. Season with sea salt to taste and serve as an appetizer. This beet tart goes well with a simple salad of mixed greens.

Note: Beets and goat cheese are a classic combination, but you may wish to use feta or blue cheese.

Pear, Blue Cheese and Walnut
Puff Pastry Tart

For years a pear, blue cheese and walnut savory loaf has been a staple for my brunches. That recipe isn't difficult to make but it requires some preparation, like measuring flour, shredding cheese and mixing a batter. I took the traditional flavors and textures of the loaf and turned them into a simple tart. Using a roll of frozen puff pastry makes this appetizer really simple to make. I like serving this tart with a balsamic glaze, which you can find in the cheese aisle of your supermarket.

Makes one 9 x 13-inch (23 x 33-cm) tart

2 large Bosc pears

½ cup (60 g) blue cheese

½ cup (58 g) walnuts

1 sheet puff pastry, defrosted

1 cup (36 g) mixed greens (optional)

1–2 tsp (5–10 ml) balsamic glaze (optional)

Preheat the oven to 375°F (190°C). It's better to have all the ingredients ready before you get the puff pastry out of the fridge, in order to keep it as cold as possible. Halve each pear, spoon out the core and thinly slice each half. Measure out the blue cheese and crumble it. Either roughly chop the walnuts or break them with your fingers—I usually find this easier for a smaller quantity of nuts.

Once all the ingredients are prepared, take the puff pastry out of the fridge and unroll it. If it's rolled in parchment paper, then keep the pastry on it. If you are using the kind that doesn't come wrapped in anything, then place it on a piece of parchment paper. Using a rolling pin dusted with some flour, lightly roll the pastry to make it a little bit bigger. Transfer the rolled-out sheet of puff pastry to a baking sheet that is 9 x 13 inches (23 x 33 cm) or larger.

Arrange the pear slices over the puff pastry. Arrange them all in rows or, alternatively, fan out pear slices in each of the four corners for a more rustic look. Scatter the crumbled blue cheese and chopped walnuts evenly over the pear slices.

Bake in the oven for 20 to 25 minutes. If using, sprinkle fresh mixed greens over the baked tart and drizzle with some balsamic glaze.

Note: I love adding fresh greens to this tart for a complete appetizer or even a light lunch. You can find balsamic glaze in most grocery stores either in the cheese section or near the oil and vinegar.

PASTRAMI-STYLE *Chicken Breast*

This is a Russian recipe that I adapted over the years. Like many Russian recipes, it didn't have exact measurements. The instructions were to use a little bit of this and that, to taste. It's also not real pastrami, but that is how the recipe was named when I learned it, and it uses a few similar techniques, such as brining and cooking at a high temperature. The recipe is really easy, but takes a little bit of preparation as the chicken needs a couple of hours to brine and then a few hours to cook and cool in the oven. In the end, you get delicious deli-style chicken. It's not going to be juicy or moist, but it's not supposed to be. Use it for sandwiches or impress your guests by creating a simple cheese and charcuterie platter with your homemade deli meat.

Makes 2 chicken breasts

BRINE
1 liter water

2 tbsp (30 g) salt

2 chicken breasts (about 1 lb [455 g])

SPICE RUB
1 tsp smoked paprika

1 tsp sweet paprika

½ tsp cayenne pepper

1 tsp garlic powder

¼ tsp salt (though I prefer to use less)

¼ tsp pepper

1 tbsp (15 ml) olive oil

In a large bowl, combine the water and salt, and mix until the salt dissolves. Submerge the chicken breasts in the salt solution, cover the bowl and let the chicken brine on a counter for 1 to 2 hours.

Preheat the oven to 500°F (260°C). Line a small roasting pan with foil as it'll make the cleanup easier. In a small bowl, combine all the seasonings and the olive oil to make a paste. Take the chicken breasts out of the brining solution, pat dry with a paper towel and smear them with the seasoning paste all over. Place in the prepared roasting pan. Make sure that the oven is actually fully preheated, as reaching 500°F (260°C) takes a long time. Put the roasting pan in the oven and roast for 20 minutes. Turn the oven off and let the chicken cool in the oven for another 2 hours. Do not open the oven. Once cooled, slice and serve.

Note: If you can find a small turkey breast that is about 1 pound (455 g), you can use it to make pastrami-style turkey breast.

SHEET PAN BEAN AND CORN *Nachos*

I love pub food: jalapeño poppers, fried cheese sticks, nachos. Of course, nachos. My nachos of choice are simple. Never with chicken or pulled pork. Always with sour cream and avocado. In this recipe, I add black beans and corn for extra texture, protein and flavor. Everything is baked on a sheet pan and comes out of the oven ready to eat. Just add your favorite toppings and enjoy.

Serves 4

4 cups (135 g) corn chips

½ jalapeño (or more if you prefer spicier food)

1 cup (145 g) canned corn, drained

1 cup (255 g) canned black beans, rinsed

2 tsp (5 g) taco seasoning

1 cup (120 g) shredded cheddar

1 cup (120 g) shredded Monterey Jack cheese with jalapeños

Jalapeños, guacamole, cilantro, sour cream, salsa, lime and lemon wedges for serving

Preheat the oven to 400°F (204°C). Evenly spread the corn chips on a sheet pan that is 9 x 13 inches (23 x 33 cm, a quarter sheet pan). Remove seeds and white ribs from the jalapeño pepper and finely dice it. Make sure to either use gloves when handling the jalapeño pepper or wash your hands really well a few times after. Scatter the jalapeño, corn and black beans over the chips. Then sprinkle with your favorite taco seasoning. Cover with the shredded cheese.

Bake for 10 to 15 minutes or until the cheese is all melted. Serve with sour cream, your choice of salsa, guacamole, cilantro, lime or lemon wedges and extra jalapeños.

Note: It's not necessary to measure out the corn chips—just use enough to cover the sheet pan in one layer. To make this appetizer a little bit healthier, you can use half the cheese.

EASY ROMESCO *Sauce*

Traditionally, Romesco sauce is made with roasted peppers and almonds, and thickened with stale bread. I love the sweet, buttery taste of toasted pecans, so I use them instead of almonds. Balsamic vinegar adds a little extra sweetness to the sauce also. The sauce is thick and creamy, so it's hard to believe that there's no cream in it. Feel free to add more salt, extra cayenne and even smoked paprika for a more piquant flavor.

Makes about 1 cup (245 g)

2 large red bell peppers

1 medium tomato

4 cloves garlic

1 thick slice of Italian bread (about 30 g [1 oz])

2 tbsp (30 ml) olive oil, divided

¼ cup (30 g) pecan halves

½ tbsp (7 ml) balsamic vinegar

½ tsp paprika

¼ tsp cayenne pepper (optional)

¼ tsp salt, or more to taste

Extra olive oil to drizzle on top (optional)

Preheat the oven to 400°F (204°C). Cut the peppers in half and remove the seeds and white ribs. Halve the tomato and cut out the stem part. Arrange the peppers and tomato cut-side up on a roasting pan or a baking sheet. I use one that is 9 x 13 inches (23 x 33 cm). Add the garlic and bread to the pan. Drizzle 1 tablespoon (15 ml) of olive oil over everything and place in the oven. Put pecans into a smaller baking dish and place in the oven as well.

After 10 minutes, remove the pecans and the toasted slice of bread and set aside. Return the rest of the veggies to the oven for another 15 minutes.

After 15 minutes, carefully flip the tomatoes and peppers. I like covering the garlic cloves with one of the pepper halves at this point. It prevents the garlic from burning. Return the veggies to the oven for another 30 minutes, or until the peppers are well charred and soft.

Once cooked, remove the pan from the oven, transfer the peppers to a bowl and cover it tightly with a piece of plastic wrap to help the skin on the peppers loosen. After about 20 to 30 minutes, uncover the peppers and peel the skin off. Peel the tomato skin off as well.

Add the peppers, tomatoes, garlic, pecans and the slice of toasted bread (torn into chunks) to a food processor. Process for about 2 to 3 minutes until a thick sauce forms. Add the remaining 1 tablespoon (15 ml) of olive oil, balsamic vinegar, paprika, cayenne and salt to taste. Pulse for a few more seconds to combine.

Drizzle with extra olive oil once in a serving dish, if desired. Serve with toasted bread or fresh vegetables.

Delicious and Unique Desserts

I love cooking, but baking is my true passion. I started out making fancy layered cakes with mousses and meringues, but over the years, my baking style has changed, and I now gravitate towards simple one-layer cakes or quick breads. I feel like no dinner is complete without a morsel of something sweet to have with a cup of tea or coffee in the end. The smell of caramelizing sugar and the wafts of cinnamon that fill the kitchen make me forget all troubles.

There's something alchemical in the transformation of butter, sugar and flour into delicious cakes and pies. I love the scientific precision that is required to make a dessert. For this book, I decided to forgo the most traditional muffins, tartlets and pastries in favor of a few more unique recipes that showcase the use of the oven even more than other common sweets. Baked Apples Stuffed with Prunes and Pecans (page 161) and Russian-Style Apple-Blueberry Jam (page 166) are traditional Russian desserts with some twists. I took the most common Russian cake and stuffed it into peaches (Cake-Stuffed Peaches, page 165) for an elegant dessert.

Fruit is often overlooked in desserts and is used mostly as a filling for pies, tarts and muffins. I love making it the star of the recipes. Roasted Pears Stuffed with Ricotta (page 157) is one of the simplest desserts you can make, yet it's gorgeous and so delicious that it could be served at a fancy dinner (or breakfast, if you like sweets in the morning). Roasted Berries with Orange Mascarpone (page 170) adds a touch of whimsy to a mixture of simple roasted berries and there's very little that could be more satisfying than the melting texture of caramelized bananas in the Roasted Cinnamon Bananas (page 169).

Stunning Strawberry *Slab Cake*

For years, I used to make a strawberry meringue cake in the summer. It was such a delicious dessert, but it took a long time to make. I had to separate the eggs and make meringue, which was then covered with half of the frozen and grated dough. The cake looked impressive and tasted delicious, but I could not make myself bake it more than once a year. So, finally, I decided to make a variation of that dessert. I liked the cake part of the recipe but I wanted it to be a bit softer, so I added ricotta to it. I then completely removed the meringue and kept the cake simple. The result is gorgeous, delicious and super easy. You only need one bowl to mix all the ingredients and one pan to bake the cake.

Makes one 9 x 13-inch (23 x 33-cm) cake

1 stick (½ cup [115 g]) unsalted butter, room temperature

1 large egg

¾ cup (145 g) sugar

¼ cup (60 g) ricotta

½ tsp vanilla extract

Pinch of salt

1½ cups (185 g) all-purpose flour

¾ tsp baking powder

1 lb (455 g) strawberries

3-4 mint leaves (optional)

Preheat the oven to 350°F (176°C). Generously butter and flour a quarter sheet pan or a baking form that is 9 x 13 inches (23 x 33 cm).

Using a hand-held mixer, mix together the butter, egg and sugar until smooth. Add the ricotta, vanilla and salt; mix well. Add the flour and baking powder, and mix on low speed until a soft dough forms. You don't have to use a hand-held mixer and can mix everything with a spatula, but a mixer makes the process easier and faster.

Using your hands, spread the dough evenly onto the pan. If at that point the oven is not fully preheated, then place the pan with the dough in the fridge.

Hull and thinly slice the strawberries. I like using a strawberry slicer as it only takes a few minutes to slice the whole pound of strawberries with the gadget.

Once the oven is preheated, take the prepared pan with the dough out of the fridge and bake for 20 minutes without the fruit. After 20 minutes, take the pan out and gently press the dough with the back of a spoon to flatten it a bit. Evenly spread the sliced strawberries over the cake and return to the oven for another 40 minutes.

Roll the mint leaves into a tight roll and thinly slice. Once the cake is baked, take it out of the oven and sprinkle the sliced mint leaves over the cake. Enjoy warm or cool.

Note: Mint leaves are optional, but I highly recommend them. They add a tiny bit of freshness and coolness to the cake and are a welcome flavor contrast to the strawberries. As a variation, you can add mangos to the cake. I made it once with 1 pound (455 g) of strawberries mixed with 1 chopped mango.

Roasted Pears STUFFED WITH RICOTTA

I love baking with ricotta. I think it's my Russian roots speaking. There's a similar dairy product that is very popular in Russia called farmer cheese (*tvorog*) and there are hundreds of desserts featuring this smooth and delicious ingredient. It's not as common in North America, so I usually use ricotta when I crave that familiar farmer cheese flavor. In this recipe I paired ricotta with almonds to create a cheesecake-like filling.

Serves 1 to 2

1 Bosc pear

¼ cup (60 g) smooth ricotta

½ tsp cinnamon

2 tbsp (10 g) ground almonds

½ tsp maple syrup (optional)

⅛ tsp almond extract (optional)

1 tbsp (7 g) sliced almonds

Preheat the oven to 350°F (176°C). While the oven is preheating, prepare the pear. Cut it in half lengthwise. Using a melon baller, scoop out the core and seeds, and discard. Scoop out more flesh from the center of the pear, leaving about ⅓ inch (8 mm) on each side. You'll end up with approximately ¼ cup (45 g) of scooped-out pear.

Mash the scooped-out pear with a fork. I find that it's easier to do right on the cutting board. Don't worry if it's not fully smooth; you just don't want the pear to be in big pieces. In a small bowl, mix together the mashed pear, ricotta, cinnamon, ground almonds, maple syrup and almond extract, if using. I like a little bit of extra sweetness, so I add ½ teaspoon of maple syrup, but if the pears you are using are sweet enough, you may omit it.

Slice a very small sliver off the bottom of the pears so that they don't roll on the pan. Divide the mixture in half and place back into the scooped-out pear halves. Sprinkle with sliced almonds. Put the pear halves ricotta-side up onto a roasting pan and bake in the oven for 20 minutes. Enjoy warm.

Note: If you don't have a melon baller, don't worry; you can use a small ice cream scoop or the sharp edge of a spoon. I find that plastic spoons work best in this case. This recipe can be easily doubled, tripled or more—just increase all the ingredients proportionally.

BAKED *Milk*

This is a really fun and unique old Russian recipe. When milk is baked in the oven for a long time, a lot of moisture evaporates and sugars concentrate. Baked milk comes out much thicker than regular milk, almost like cream. It has a caramel color and sweet, almost caramel taste. It also has a lot more calories, so it's perfect to give to kids as dessert. It tastes absolutely delicious warm just out of the oven, but I love it cold also. I like adding it to my Millet Porridge with Cranberries (page 20) or just drinking it straight in small portions.

Makes ¾ cup (180 ml)

2 cups (480 ml) 2% milk

Preheat the oven to 325°F (163°C). While the oven is preheating, pour the milk into a stovetop and ovenproof pot. Bring the milk to a boil, and then place the pot into the fully preheated oven. Alternatively, you can use a stovetop pot to bring the milk to boil and then pour it into a baking dish.

Bake uncovered for 2½ to 3 hours. Then turn the oven off and let the milk cool in the oven, about another 2 hours.

Once the milk is baked, it will be covered by a thick and very brown skin. You can discard it, but I like keeping a few pieces and eating them; it's almost like milk leather. Strain the milk and enjoy it.

It will keep in the fridge for 2 to 3 days.

Note: Use a regular stainless steel ovenproof pot or a ceramic baking dish. Cast iron pans and Dutch ovens conduct heat a lot better, so the milk will evaporate almost completely in 2½ to 3 hours.

Baked Apples STUFFED WITH PRUNES AND PECANS

Growing up, baked apples were a very popular afternoon treat in my family. My grandma made delicious cakes and pies, but if I wanted something sweet on a busy day then she'd make a few baked apples for me. Now, whenever I make baked apples, I transport just for a moment to the past, to the time of childhood innocence, a warm kitchen with aromas of cinnamon and my grandma asking me if I want another helping.

This recipe is perfect any time of the year. It's great in the fall when apples are harvested and the smells of spices are in the cool air. It's a warming dessert for the cold winter months and it's delicious in the spring and summer when you don't want to bake a whole apple pie but crave that familiar apple pie flavor.

Serves 6

6 large apples (I use Ambrosia, but you can use your favorite baking apples such as Honeycrisp or Golden Delicious)

Juice of ½ lemon, divided

⅓ cup (38 g) roughly chopped pecans

⅓ cup (50 g) chopped prunes (about 4 prunes)

¾ tsp cinnamon

½ tbsp (7 g) butter (you can use vegan butter)

1 tsp brown sugar (optional, depending on the sweetness of the apples)

Preheat the oven to 350°F (176°C). While the oven is preheating, prepare the apples. If you have a special corer tool, it'll make your job easier. I usually use a sharp paring knife to cut out the top part and a teaspoon to scrape the middle of the apple out. You don't need to scrape a lot, maybe about an inch (2.5 cm) wide and 1½ inch (3.8 cm) deep. Discard whatever you scraped out, or eat it as a healthy snack.

Immediately squeeze a little bit of lemon juice inside the cored apples to prevent browning.

In a small bowl, mix together the pecans, prunes, cinnamon and any lemon juice you have left. Mix well, and spoon the mixture into the cored apples. About one spoon of mixture each. Top with a pea-size pat of butter and a sprinkling of brown sugar, if using.

Place the apples onto a rimmed baking sheet or roasting pan and bake for 45 to 60 minutes. I prefer a much softer apple texture so I usually bake them for an hour. If you prefer firmer apples, then 45 minutes should be enough.

Note: You can vary the filling if you'd like. You can use pecans and dates, almonds and dried apricots. You can use raisins, dried cherries or dried cranberries if you like. You can even omit dried fruit if that's your preference.

SIMPLE APRICOT AND PLUM *Cobbler*

Sun-kissed apricots and navy-colored plums are one of the last fruits of the summer. They are usually ripe and ready for picking at the end of August, right around the time when the stores drag out plastic pumpkins for their shelves, and the air smells like cinnamon and cloves in all the coffee shops. In this dessert, I combine the summer bounty with my favorite fall flavors of pumpkin and cinnamon. You can't really taste the pumpkin in this cobbler; it acts like an egg in the dough and makes this dessert just a tiny bit more nutritious.

Serves 4

½ lb (227 g) apricots (about 5 medium)

½ lb (227 g) blue plums (about 5 plums)

¼ cup (30 g) all-purpose flour

¼ cup (20 g) quick-cooking oats

¼ cup (20 g) ground almonds

¼ cup (55 g) light brown sugar

1 tsp baking powder

¼ tsp salt

2 tsp (5 g) cinnamon

¼ cup (60 g) cold unsalted butter

¼ cup (45 g) pumpkin puree

Whipped cream for serving

Preheat the oven to 350°F (176°C). Pit and quarter the apricots and plums. Cover the bottom of a 1-liter baking dish with the prepared fruit.

In a medium bowl, combine all the dry ingredients and spices and whisk together. Cut the butter into small pieces and add to the dry ingredients. Using a fork or a pastry knife, mix the butter into the dry ingredients until the mixture resembles coarse sand. You can also use a food processor: just pulse a few times until the butter is mixed in and is no bigger than pea size. Add the pumpkin puree and mix until a soft dough forms.

Spread the dough over the fruit and bake in the oven for about 40 minutes, until the cobbler topping is baked through and the fruit under the topping is bubbly. Serve with whipped cream.

Note: I love desserts that aren't overly sweet, and I find that the slight tanginess in the fruit works beautifully with the sweet cobbler topping. If you prefer sweeter desserts, add about 2 to 3 spoonfuls of brown sugar to the fruit and mix.

CAKE-STUFFED *Peaches*

One of the most common Russian cakes is called *sharlotka*. Just like apple pie, it has many different variations. Some recipes use sour cream, some separate the eggs and some add oil. The recipe that my mom makes is very simple. It just has eggs, sugar, flour and fruit—most often apples. I like making mine with peaches or nectarines.

These cake-stuffed peaches are a healthier variation of that traditional *sharlotka*. I took the basic batter from the cake and added it into the pitted peaches. You still get the familiar taste but in an individual serving. I recommend eating these peaches the same day, as the cake part will get a little soggy from all the delicious peach juices if left overnight.

Serves 3 to 6

3 large peaches

1 large egg

3 tbsp (35 g) sugar

¼ cup (30 g) all-purpose flour

1 tbsp (15 g) plain yogurt

¼ tsp baking powder

Small pinch of salt

Preheat the oven to 375°F (190°C). Halve and pit the peaches. Scoop out a little bit of flesh from the peaches to make space for the cake stuffing. Make the cake batter. In a small bowl, whisk together the egg and sugar until just incorporated. No need to whip it to double its size, only whisk together for 30 to 45 seconds. Add the flour, yogurt, baking powder and salt. Mix together until a thick batter forms.

Spoon the batter into the scooped-out peaches. Place the peaches onto a roasting pan and bake for 1 hour. You might need to cover the roasting pan with foil after about 45 minutes if the cake stuffing begins to brown too much, so check periodically.

Serve warm or at room temperature. These cake-stuffed peaches don't keep well, so it's better to eat them the same day. Otherwise, the juices from the peach will make the cake soggy.

Note: Optionally, add some cardamom to the batter; it complements the peach flavor really well.

Russian-Style Apple-Blueberry *Jam*

Russian-style jam is called *varenye*. It has similar ingredients to traditional jam—fruit and sugar—but has a different texture. The preserves are chunkier and often have whole fruit in thick syrup. There are even *varenye* that are made from whole young walnuts in shells or pine cones. Just like regular jams, Russian-style jams take a long time to prepare and often require a lot of stirring to make sure that the sugar doesn't crystallize.

Making the jam in the oven means that you don't have to spend hours stooping over a steaming pot. All the ingredients are simply added to an ovenproof dish and left to the mercy of the oven. In the end, you get almost translucent pieces of apples suspended in blueberry-colored sugar syrup. Eat it with a spoon as a dessert, spoon over pancakes or ice cream, or spread over buttered toast for a delicious, albeit indulgent, breakfast.

Makes about ³⁄₄ cup (180 ml)

2 small Gala apples (½ lb [227 g])

⅔ cup (100 g) frozen blueberries

1 small cinnamon stick (optional)

½ tsp cinnamon

⅓ cup (65 g) white sugar

Preheat the oven to 450°F (232°C). While the oven is preheating, quarter each apple and remove the core and seeds. Chop the apples into ¼-inch (6-mm) pieces. Place the chopped apples into a shallow, ovenproof baking dish with about 1-liter capacity or a small, ovenproof pot. Add the frozen blueberries and cinnamon stick, sprinkle with the cinnamon and add the sugar on top. Do not mix.

Place the baking dish into the oven and cook for 40 minutes. After 40 minutes, carefully mix with a spoon, reduce the heat to 400°F (204°C) and return to the oven for another 40 minutes.

This jam tastes great on buttered toast. It will last in the fridge for about a week.

Note: This is a Russian-style jam, which is chunky with pieces of fruit in syrup. In Russia, jams are often eaten as a dessert with a spoon or as an accompaniment to tea.

ROASTED CINNAMON *Bananas*

Many years ago, my husband and I went to Costa Rica for our honeymoon. One of the places where we stopped had a cook who served homemade food and spoke very little English. One night, she made an incredible dessert with sticky and caramelized bananas. It was amazing, so I asked her to repeat it the next day. "It's impossible," she said. The next evening, dessert included bananas, a lot of sugar and even butter—all the ingredients for caramelized bananas—but it wasn't what I wanted, and I was incredibly disappointed. Since then, the expression "impossible bananas" has become a staple in our vocabulary. We use it often whenever something obvious and easy cannot happen for unknown reasons. This recipe is a healthier version of that delectable dessert.

Serves 2 to 4

2 tsp (9 g) coconut oil, not melted, divided

1 tbsp (15 ml) maple syrup

2 large ripe bananas

1 tsp cinnamon

1 tbsp (14 g) brown sugar

Preheat the oven to 400°F (204°C). Brush a small 7 x 11-inch (18 x 28-cm) roasting pan with 1 teaspoon of coconut oil. You just need it to be big enough to hold all the bananas. Pour the maple syrup onto the bottom of the dish, and brush it on top of the coconut oil.

Slice each banana in half lengthwise and then cut each half into thirds. You'll end up with 12 pieces. Place the bananas onto the roasting pan, cut-side up. Evenly sprinkle with the cinnamon. I like using a little sieve to create an even layer. Sprinkle with the brown sugar. Dot each banana with the remaining coconut oil.

Bake for 15 minutes. Once cooked, turn the bananas over in the syrup a couple of times and serve. This is great hot with some ice cream. You can add them to yogurt and serve with Easy Cranberry-Pecan Granola (page 16). You can also eat them on their own as a delicious dessert.

Note: You may also use an 8- to 9-inch (20- to 23-cm) pie plate.

ROASTED BERRIES WITH ORANGE *Mascarpone*

Just like many of my recipes, this one was born out of necessity. I was cleaning out my freezer before the birth of my daughter and found a few half-empty bags of frozen berries. I'm not a big smoothie fan and making a pie seemed too daunting at that point, so I threw all the berries together in a roasting pan, added a bit of orange juice and some cornstarch to slightly thicken the sauce, and a delicious, light and easy dessert was created. Months later I added mascarpone cream to make this recipe a bit more special and festive. Serve it in a big roasting pan, family style, at the end of dinner, or in individual ramekins.

Serves 4

Zest of 1 medium navel orange, divided

Juice of 1 medium navel orange, divided

¼ cup (60 g) mascarpone

1 tbsp (15 ml) maple syrup, or more to taste

2 tbsp (20 g) cornstarch

3 cups (445 g) frozen mixed berries

Preheat the oven to 350°F (176°C). Prepare 4 small ramekins or one small roasting pan, about 1-quart (1-liter) in size. In a small bowl, mix together half the zest, 2 teaspoons (10 ml) of orange juice and mascarpone until smooth. Optionally, add 1 to 2 teaspoons (5 to 10 ml) of maple syrup to sweeten the mascarpone.

In a medium bowl, mix together the rest of the orange juice with the cornstarch until the cornstarch dissolves. Add the rest of the zest, maple syrup and frozen berries; mix well. Pour the berry mixture into the ramekins or the roasting pan and bake for 30 minutes.

After half an hour, the juices will thicken slightly and the berries will become soft and luscious. Serve with generous dollops of orange mascarpone.

Note: Feel free to add extra maple syrup to the fruit if you prefer a sweeter dessert. I made this with frozen strawberries, blueberries and raspberries. I once added frozen cherries to the mix and also tried it with strawberries only.

Mango and Black Currants
Fruit Leather

When I moved to Canada and went to high school, I watched in fascination as my classmates unrolled brightly colored fruit leather during lunch recess. I had never seen or tried anything like this. Then, I was on a mission to become familiar with this snack, but was soon disappointed. The texture was fun and chewy, but the flavor was just one-dimensional: sweet. Years later, when the Internet exploded with all things food related, I came across a recipe for fruit leather and immediately became fascinated again. As it turned out, fruit leather is not difficult to prepare but requires time and patience. Fruit puree—sometimes slightly sweetened, sometimes not—is spread on parchment paper and then dried out for hours until almost no moisture remains. It's a delicious snack or dessert, and it's healthy when made at home. I love using black currants from my garden. I urge you to try and find them at your farmers' market in the summer—the flavor is very unique and works well with mango.

Makes 8 small servings

1 cup (165 g) mango (1 large fruit, about ½ lb [227 g])

½ cup (75 g) black currants

1 tsp maple syrup

Preheat the oven to 175°F (79°C). If your oven doesn't heat this low, then 200°F (93°C) will also work. Cover a sheet pan that is 9 x 13 inches (23 x 33 cm) with parchment paper. In a small food processor, pulse the mango until very smooth and spread it thinly onto the prepared sheet pan. In the same food processor, blend the black currants really well. Strain the black currant puree through a sieve to remove all the skins. You'll end up with only a little bit of the smooth puree; add the maple syrup to it and mix. Dot the black currant puree over the mango and spread it with a spatula to create a marbling effect.

Dry the fruit mixture in the oven for about 3 hours. If the air is humid, it may take a little longer. After 3 hours, remove the fruit leather and touch it. It should be tacky but not sticky. Bake for another 15 to 30 minutes if it's too sticky.

Once the fruit leather is cooked, transfer the parchment paper to a cutting board and cut the uneven edges of the fruit leather with a sharp knife. Roll the fruit leather together with the parchment along the long side, as if you were to roll sushi. Cut the roll into 8 pieces and serve. Alternatively, you can roll the fruit leather without the parchment and then individually wrap each piece.

Note: If you can't find black currants, you can use blueberries. Omit the maple syrup and add a bit of lemon juice instead.

Equipment

You don't need anything fancy or really expensive to create delicious and easy meals in your oven, but there are a few things that will make your life a lot easier:

1.   Oven thermometer. I can't stress enough how important it is. Whether you have an oven like mine that doesn't come with any digital displays, or an electric oven with temperatures showing on the panel, it's crucial to make sure that the oven is actually properly preheated. I use a no-frills thermometer that has really great reviews: the CDN High Heat Oven Thermometer.

2.   Meat thermometer. This is another item that I cannot cook meat without. I am extremely paranoid about undercooking chicken or other meats. In fact, I personally prefer to overcook meats by about 10 degrees just to be on the safe side. I never blindly follow a recipe. It may say to cook chicken for 30 minutes, but after the allotted time I will always check the doneness with the meat thermometer. If it's not cooked through to the correct temperature, I leave it in the oven longer. I use Lavatools Thermowand.

3.   Sheet pans. Personally, I prefer nonstick, as they are really easy to clean and require less oil. If you clean them right away, they will keep well for a couple of years. However, they will get oils and butters stuck to them and will eventually need to be replaced. I also have aluminum and steel sheet pans; they work just as well and you can scrape them, so cleaning is easier.

4.   Measuring cups and spoons. You can buy them anywhere and they don't have to be expensive. I've seen Betty Crocker brand at various dollar stores. You can also get cute ones at IKEA. I cook so much that I have four sets of measuring cups and three sets of measuring spoons.

1 cup = 240 ml

1 tablespoon = 15 ml

1 teaspoon = 5 ml

5.   Scale. A lot of my recipes also have weight measurements. I know, for example, that ½ cup of shredded cheddar is about 60 grams (a little bit under 2 ounces), so it's a lot easier to just cut out 60 grams from a block of cheese than randomly shredding cheese and measuring with a cup. It's also a lot easier to measure broccoli by weight than trying to add broccoli florets into cups. You can get a kitchen scale easily on Amazon for about 15 to 20 dollars. I've had mine for about a decade and it's still working great.

Safe Internal Cooking Temperatures

United States standards (as defined by the United Stated Department of Agriculture [USDA]):

Ground meat (non poultry) - 160°F (71°C)

Ground meat (poultry) - 165°F (74°C)

Meats - 145°F (63°C)

Poultry - 165°F (74°C)

Fish - 145°F (63°C)

Canadian standards (as defined by Health Canada):

Ground meats - 165°F (74°C)

Meats - 160°F (71°C)

Poultry (pieces) - 165°F (74°C)

Poultry (whole) - 180°F (82°C)

Fish - 158°F (70°C)

Check online for more information about minimum safe internal cooking temperatures. I am extremely paranoid about undercooking meats—I almost always cook food for a bit longer so that the internal temperature is higher.

Acknowledgments

I laughed out loud and rolled my eyes when I received an email in April 2017 with the subject line "Imagelicious cookbook." There was no way that it wouldn't be one of dozens of spam emails I got every week. I almost clicked delete without reading it but decided to indulge myself. My heart skipped a beat when I realized that the email sounded legitimate. I quickly checked the email address and that, too, seemed real. It was too good to be true, but it was true.

I'd like to thank Page Street Publishing: Marissa, Meg, Carrie Bond and, of course, Will for believing in me and giving me this amazing opportunity to write a cookbook. Your guidance, advice and trust have been instrumental in making it happen. Thank you for making my dream come true—a dream I thought I would never be able to achieve, a dream that I was afraid to admit to myself I even had.

This book wouldn't be possible without my amazing recipe testers, who not only provided me with valuable feedback, but also gave me confidence when I felt unsure of myself. Thank you Olya, Marina, Gloria, Elmi, Ilona, Melissa, Diana, Amanda, Selena and Jamilya. I'm grateful that you believed in me and in my recipes!

I spent many days and long hours deciding if writing a cookbook is something I should pursue. The amount of work felt monumental, and I wasn't sure if it was a good fit for me at a time in my life when I was staying home with an infant. My family was very enthusiastic about this opportunity, except for my grandma who, for some unknown reason, didn't share this excitement in the beginning (I'm happy that she got over her initial hesitation). Thanks to my dad and stepmom for assuring me that it is something I should and could do. Thanks to my sisters, brother and sister-in-law for being overly happy and thrilled about my cookbook, perhaps even more than I was.

Thank you to my second family, my family-in-law, who always praise my cooking and make me blush a little bit from all their compliments. You are my favorite people to cook for as you love everything I make!

Heartfelt thanks to my grandparents, who are sadly no longer here and won't ever know that I wrote a cookbook. Their love of food is what made me love cooking in the first place. My grandma was an amazing cook: She loved her garden and grew vegetables and fruits that nourished us throughout long winters. Once my grandparents moved to Canada, Grandpa also started learning to cook. I still have a stack of cooking magazines with his notes. He loved trying new dishes and was always proud to share them with me. When I started cooking and baking, my grandparents encouraged me and believed in me. I wouldn't be the cook I am today without their support, and for that, I am eternally grateful. I miss you both every day.

Thank you to my dear mom who is my number one fan. Thank you for never making me do chores when I was little and for just letting me be in the kitchen with you when you cooked. I watched and observed all the time. In the end, I learned that cooking is not a chore, it's a privilege. I am lucky enough to be able to go to a store and buy any ingredient I need for a recipe. That wasn't the case 30 years ago in the Soviet Union. Thank you, Mom, for loving me unconditionally and believing in me. Thank you for babysitting and constantly asking questions about the book. Thank you for being you. I love you!

Thank you to my adorable daughter, Lana, who graciously decided to learn to crawl just two weeks before my deadline to finish developing and photographing all the recipes. If you crawled earlier, I wouldn't have been able to do everything in time. Thank you for just sitting where I plopped you and staying in one spot.

And, of course, thank you to my husband, Alan. Without your support, your encouragement, your help, I physically wouldn't have been able to write this book. You are the constant in my life. You are my rock. You are my life (even when I roll my eyes at you). Words cannot describe how happy I am that I met you and how grateful I am every day of my life that we chose each other. I love you more than you know!

About the Author

Julia's love for food started at a young age when she spent summers at the cottage with her grandparents, watching them grow fruits and vegetables and raise chickens. She was born in Russia and moved to Canada when she was a teenager. After graduating from university, she started experimenting with cooking and baking. Her love for baking led Julia to embark on a year-long journey to complete a Bakery Arts evening program at George Brown College and receive a Bakery Arts Certificate.

After a few years of scribbling recipes on post-its and loose sheets of paper, Julia started her website, Imagelicious, where she began writing down her favorite recipes along with some memories, stories and notes. Cooking and baking turned into a passion, which in turn sparked a love of photography. Julia returned once again to George Brown College to take a few courses on photography and writing. Now, Julia's photographs can be found on the menus of a few Toronto restaurants.

Julia lives in Toronto with her husband and adorable daughter.

Index